Student Perceptions of Outdoor Educational Expe

by

Cynthia Edlund

CW01499744

M.S., University of Wisconsin – Stevens Point, 2001

B.S., Colorado State University – Pueblo, 1988

Doctoral Study Submitted in Partial Fulfillment

of the Requirements for the Degree of

Doctor of Education

The Teacher as Leader

Walden University

January 2011

Walden University

COLLEGE OF EDUCATION

This is to certify that the doctoral study by

Cynthia Edlund

has been found to be complete and satisfactory in all respects,
and that any and all revisions required by
the review committee have been made.

Review Committee
Dr. Colin Winkelman, Committee Chairperson, Education Faculty
Dr. Christina Dawson, Committee Member, Education Faculty
Dr. Wallace Southerland, University Reviewer, Education Faculty

Chief Academic Officer

David Clinefelter, Ph.D.

Walden University
2011

Abstract

Student Perceptions of Outdoor Educational Experiences

by

Cynthia Edlund

M.S., University of Wisconsin – Stevens Point, 2001

B.S., Colorado State University – Pueblo, 1988

Doctoral Study Submitted in Partial Fulfillment

of the Requirements for the Degree of

Doctor of Education

The Teacher as Leader

Walden University

January 2011

Abstract

Research has underscored the importance of experiences in natural surroundings to help children thrive and indicated that students spend little to no time outdoors. Knowledge regarding how students make meaning of outdoor educational experiences is limited, and such information can help school districts understand more about the importance of providing outdoor educational experiences. The purpose of this phenomenological study was to explore the lived experiences of students who participated in outdoor educational experiences. Dewey's experiential education theory and Gardner's natural intelligence theory informed this study. Research questions elicited how students described and understood their lived experiences with outdoor education, what students recalled of those experiences, and how students saw those experiences being important to them in the future. Data from interviews with 8 recently graduated high school students were analyzed by identifying semantic relationships between frames of analysis to identify themes. Key results revealed that earliest outdoor memories were rooted in family experiences and that students recalled outdoor educational experiences embedded in a holistic, interdisciplinary environment where experiential learning stimulated cognition. Conclusions included themes of personal growth and leadership, values, and cognitive freedom. Recommendations included providing opportunities for family use of outdoor education facilities in school planning and providing professional development in the field of outdoor education. Contributions to positive social change are insights on the value of outdoor educational experiences for students and the discovery that the experiences contributed to their personal growth, enhanced their learning, and led to the development of value systems and career goals.

Dedication

This doctoral study is dedicated to Megan and Logan, who have grown into incredible adults of whom I am proud to call my children and to my grandson, Isaac, who brings joy, laughter, and inspiration to me every day.

This doctoral study is also dedicated to all my "other" children – the students I have had the privilege of teaching throughout my career. You have continually motivated me to become the very best teacher I can because you deserve nothing less!

Acknowledgements

I would like to acknowledge Dr. Kim Winkelman, who served as my doctoral committee chair. Dr. Winkelman's encouragement, patience, and insight have been a source of strength throughout this journey. His commitment and expertise contributed greatly to my studies and made my time at Walden University a positive learning experience.

I would like to thank Dr. Tina Dawson, my doctoral committee member, for her leadership and support throughout this research endeavor. Dr. Dawson provided a port in the storm for the many times I thought I would flounder on this journey.

Finally, a huge thank you to my husband, Michael for giving me the time, space, and support to do what I needed to do. The Packers and Reggae were certainly an odd combination, but I'm sure glad it turned out to be the winning one that opened up our future together!

Table of Contents

List of Tables

Section 1: Introduction to the Study

Rachel Carson encouraged her readers to view nature as an inspiration and a responsibility. Carson (1956) wrote that "those who contemplate the beauty of the earth find reserves of strength that will endure as long as life lasts" (p. 86). Informal conversations among a diverse array of people are often sprinkled with references to feeling inspired and rejuvenated after spending time outdoors. It would seem that people value time spent interacting with the natural environment. Several studies (Barnett, et al., 2006; Chawla, 2007; Dyment, 2005; Faber Taylor & Kuo, 2008; Farmer, Knapp, & Benton, 2007; Foran, 2005; Wells & Lekies, 2006) underscored the importance of providing contacts with natural surroundings to create an environment where children can thrive physically, academically and developmentally.

A 2007 study of California's youth found that almost half of the children seldom to never participated in outdoor team activities or took part in any nature activities (Public Policy Institute of California, 2007). There were definite racial/ethnic differences. Twice as many Latino children did not participate in outdoor team activities or take part in any nature activities as white children. The study found that socioeconomic status also made a difference. Children whose parents made less than $40,000 were half as likely to spend time in natural surroundings. In addition, a Kaiser Family Foundation study documented that children spent more time indoors and interacted with electronic media more than did their parents. Telephone interviews revealed that children seemed to know more about the fictional worlds of electronic characters than they did about the organisms that inhabit their own world (Vandewater, et al., 2007). Hofferth and Sandberg (2001) found that when children ventured outdoors, their time was spent on structured activities instead of the types of free play that encourages problem-solving skills, interpersonal skills, communication skills, and creativity. In addition, they found that most of children's exposure to nature was secondary exposure like watching nature programs on television. During the traditional school day, children are often found inside the four walls of their classrooms. In some instances, schools utilized outdoor classrooms as an educational resource.

Outdoor classrooms have been promoted as an educational resource for many years. Dewey (1938) proposed the theory of experiential education which used sensory information from the natural world to increase the learning of children. He believed that traditional lecture methods were ineffective and that hands-on experiences along with the communication of the new understandings were essential to academic engagement. Dewey's experiential model took students out of the traditional classroom into natural settings that encouraged genuine tasks in natural settings. A natural setting "offers all children an especially salient and dramatic focus for developing the capacities to know, label, and classify, which are basic to the first stage of cognitive maturation" (Kellert, 2005, p. 68). According to Dewey's experiential model, outdoor educational experiences provide a developmentally appropriate and effective method to educate children.

In an attempt to counter children's lack of exposure to natural environments, the No Child Left Inside (NCLI) movement provides on-going effort to encourage education and public awareness of the importance of outdoor education and recreation in the lives of children across the United States (No Child Left Inside Coalition, 2009). This national campaign is an attempt to promote learning in the field as well as the classroom through the incorporation of outdoor education, experiential education, and place-based education. NCLI encourages the use of hands-on instruction relevant to students' lives in an attempt to increase their capacity for environmental stewardship and good citizenship. The Connecticut Department of Environmental Protection (2009) stated that the purpose of NCLI was to "help today's children re-connect with the great outdoors, while building the next generation of environmentally conscious citizens" (para 1). This movement spread throughout the country in response to the phenomenon in which children are becoming inured to artificial environments rather than the natural environment. The NCLI Coalition has pushed for federal legislation in the form of an amendment to the Elementary and Secondary Education Act to increase environmental education programs, which have been shown to get students outdoors while promoting higher-order thinking skills and increasing math and reading test scores (No Child Left Inside Coalition, 2009).

Research has underscored the importance of experiences in natural surroundings to help children thrive. Research and changes in education system practices indicate that students spend little to no time outdoors. The academic performance of students and the health of students are both issues discussed in national and local media (Athman & Monroe, 2004a; Bartosh, Ferguson, Tudor, & Taylor, 2009; Bartosh, Tudor, Taylor, & Ferguson, 2006; Lieberman, Hoody, & Lieberman, 2000; Monroe, Randall, & Crisp, 2001; Norman, Jennings, & Wahl, 2006). These studies have detailed the positive impact of environment-based education programming on academic achievement. Each of these studies explored the effects of using the environment as a tool for achieving educational goals. This is known as environment-based education. When environment-based education was compared to traditional education, an increase in performance on core academic areas such as reading, writing, and mathematics was found. In addition,

Athman and Monroe (2004b) found a positive effect on critical thinking skills and student disposition toward critical thinking when using the environment-based curriculum.

This study added to the literature because its focus was on understanding the student participants' perceptions of the value of outdoor educational experiences. The lack of research on what students think and if they consider it important to participate in outdoor educational activities directed the review of the literature found in section 2, which includes a detailed discussion on the need for connecting students to nature, educational theories supporting outdoor education, and the methodological insights driving the methodology of this study.

Problem Statement

Research has underscored the importance of experiences in natural surroundings to help children thrive (Athman & Monroe, 2004a; Bartosh, et al., 2009; Bartosh, et al., 2006; Lieberman, et al., 2000; Monroe, at al., 2001; & Norman, et al., 2006), yet research and changes in education system practices indicate that students spend little to no time outdoors (Public Policy Institute of California, 2007; Vandewater, et al., 2007). Because students spend little to no time engaged in outdoor educational activities, knowledge regarding how students make meaning of outdoor educational experiences is virtually non-existent; therefore, the lack of empirical knowledge regarding students' lived experiences in outdoor educational activities served as the educational problem for this study. A second educational problem, which inspired this study, was that schools are investigating the use of outdoor classrooms as an educational resource for the improvement of education. Through this investigation, school districts have been finding a "paucity of systematic study of the role played by childhood contact with natural systems" (Kellert, 2002, p. 118). This phenomenological study helped address the scarcity of research by providing an understanding of how outdoor educational experiences are perceived by students and how their attitudes towards learning have changed as a result of their experiences. The information related to the students' reflections and experiences can help school districts understand more about the importance of providing outdoor educational experiences.

Several districts in the state in which this study was conducted explored or were exploring the potential uses and benefits of outdoor educational activities before expanding funding for outdoor classrooms. The inspiration for this particular study was found in a rural preK-12 school district that, as a result of a land donation, owns a large tract of land available for use as an outdoor classroom. The current study provided this rural district with more information related to the investment in and importance of using the donated land as an outdoor classroom. The study drew from a similar district in which such programs have been in place for more than ten years.

Nature of the Study

Qualitative research searches for a "detailed description, seeking to represent reality through the eyes of participants and to be sensitive to the complexities of behavior and meaning in context" (Henwood & Pigeon, 1994, p. 227). This study approached the research through a constructivist philosophical paradigm. Creswell (2007) described constructivism as a search for an understanding of the world as formed through the participants' views. General characteristics of a qualitative approach included the "search for meaning and understanding, the researcher as the primary instrument of data collection and analysis, an inductive investigative strategy and a richly descriptive end product" (Merriam, 2002, p. 6) and described the qualitative foundations of this study.

The qualitative approach used in this research was hermeneutic phenomenology. Hermeneutic phenomenology seeks an understanding of a phenomenon through the composite perceptions of the lived experiences of several individuals. Van Manen (1990) described this human science research approach as an opportunity to investigate pedagogy, which is the science of teaching. "Pedagogy requires a hermeneutic ability to make interpretive sense of the phenomena of the life-world in order to see the pedagogic significance of situations and relations of living with children" (p. 2). From a phenomenological viewpoint, the way human beings experience the world is constantly questioned in an attempt to understand the world. This phenomenology explored the essence of the use of outdoor educational experiences as perceived by students who were enrolled in a school district, which features outdoor educational experiences as part of their curriculum. Data were collected from semistructured interviews with these students. The interviews were transcribed, coded, and analyzed. Data were analyzed in an attempt to interpret the students' understandings of their experiences of outdoor education and the natural environment. The analysis was based on the interpretations of the data through a holistic reflection of the participants' lived experiences, using both inductive and deductive reasoning. The methodology is presented in detail in section 3.

Research Questions

The following research questions guided this qualitative study:

1. How did students describe and understand the essence of their lived experiences with outdoor education?

2. What did students recall about their outdoor educational experiences and why did they recall those experiences?

3. How did the students see outdoor educational experiences being important to them in the future?

Purpose of the Study

The purpose of this phenomenological study was to explore the essence of meaning in the lived experiences of recent high school graduates who had taken part in outdoor educational experiences. This study increased our understanding about the importance of providing outdoor educational experiences for their students. This inquiry helped the school district inspiring this particular study and other local school districts make informed decisions on the allocation of money for educational programs. This study added to the literature because its focus is on understanding the student participants' perceptions of the value of outdoor educational experiences.

Conceptual Framework

The research questions guiding this study included an investigation of the ways students describe and understand the essence of their lived experiences with outdoor education, the types of activities students recall about their outdoor educational experiences, the reasons why they recall those experiences, and they ways in which students see these experiences being important to them in the future were developed. All of these investigations were guided by the tenets of phenomenology. The word 'how' is a key interrogative directing this type of qualitative research denoting an openness of the researcher to anything that may come to light during the data collection and analysis while acknowledging and respecting the perceptions shared through the voices of the participants. The search for answers to these research questions is guided by the conceptual framework.

The conceptual basis for this study was embedded in the essence of the lived experiences of high school seniors who participated in outdoor educational programming. Cobb (1977) wrote that "a major clue to mental and psychosocial, as well as psychological, health lies in the spontaneous and innately creative imagination of childhood" (p. 15). Cobb used the lived experiences of creative geniuses as related through biography and autobiography to develop her theory of the importance of a child's deep experience of nature to his or her adult cognition and psychological well-being. Walt Whitman expressed similar sentiments when he wrote:

> There was a child went forth every day; And the first object he look'd upon, that object he became; And that object became part of him for the day, or a certain part of the day, or for many years, or stretching cycles of years. (as cited in Cobb, p. 31)

Both Whitman and Cobb understood the importance of exploring a phenomenon through the perceptions of those who experienced them. In that tradition, this research study examined emerging themes in the data gathered during semistructured interviews with purposefully selected participants who experienced outdoor educational experiences.

The benefits of using nature as an educational tool have been and continue to be explored by learning theorists such as Howard Gardner (Moran, Kornhaber, & Gardner, 2006). Gardner's naturalist intelligence was defined as the ability to sense patterns and make connections in natural settings. He pointed out that

Naturalist intelligence involves the capacity to make consequential distinctions in nature—between one plant and another, among animals, clouds, mountains, and the like. Scientist Charles Darwin had naturalist intelligence in abundance. Most of us no longer use our naturalist intelligence to survive in the jungle or forest. But it is likely that our entire consumer culture is based on our naturalist capacity to differentiate one car make from another, one sneaker from another and the like. (Gardner, 2005, p.9)

Each student has some level of naturalist intelligence. Providing opportunities to use this intelligence may increase student achievement.

Gardner based the inclusion of a naturalist intelligence on human brain research. This research demonstrated that human beings are born with an affinity for nature but that children experience nature in a deeper, more direct manner than adults. "For young children, natural environment is an everlasting and dynamic stimulator, because children perceive the natural world through their primary perceptions, which are based on their sensory-directed experiences" (Hyun, 2000, p. 7). The provision of natural areas for children provided opportunities for sensory exploration and creative expression.

Margolin (2005) described American Indian pedagogy as a process in which children learned experientially. Margolin retold a native story reinforcing the importance of learning something as opposed to being taught something. He pointed out that one aspect of traditional pedagogy is "a need not just to 'know' but to experience. Knowledge is not just something to be stored and talked about; it's something to be lived" (p. 76). Indian pedagogy values creation stories, which are the knowledge and important life lessons found in animals, plants, and, in fact, the entire natural world. Hall (2007), founder of the National Indian Youth Leadership Project, stated:

> Indigenous educational approaches provide the foundation for learning based on context and relationship. By expanding the boundaries of the classroom through involvement with the broader community, including the environment, schools can build new relationships, validate the cultures of the young people they serve, and make learning meaningful and appropriate for our future. (p. 16)

The National Indian Youth Project used cultural and service features in conjunction with outdoor adventure and challenging experiential learning opportunities to help Indian youth succeed.

Students' first person testimonials of their remembrances of outdoor educational experiences precipitated new understandings of the how and why these experiences are personally important. Carson (1965) wrote that

> A child's world is fresh and new and beautiful, full of wonder and excitement. It is our misfortune that for most of us that clear-eyed vision, that true instinct for what is beautiful and awe-inspiring is dimmed and even lost before we reach adulthood. If I had influence with the good fairy who is supposed to preside over the christening of all children I should ask that her gift to each child in the world be a sense of wonder so indestructible that it would last throughout life, as an unfailing antidote against the boredom and disenchantments of later years, the sterile preoccupation with things that are artificial, the alienation from our sources of strength. (p. 54)

Theoretical frameworks that guided this study are further explored in section 2. Throughout the analysis of the data, key characteristics from the conceptual framework such as the importance of outdoor educational experiences as related to cognition, to psychological well-being, to creative expression, and with experiential learning were used in the development of frames of reference/conceptual categories.

Definition of Terms

In order to facilitate clarity of thought throughout this research, the following terms and definitions are provided.

Environment-based education: Often thought of as nature studies, education uses the environment as a tool for achieving educational goals. It emphasizes interdisciplinary integration of subject matter and constructivist learning using the environment as a focus on which to build curriculum (Ernst & Monroe, 2006).

Environmental Education: The United States Environmental Protection Agency (2009) defined environmental education as gaining "an understanding of how individual actions affect the environment, acquire skills to weight various sides of issues, and become better equipped to make informed decisions" (para. 1).

Lived Experiences: Dilthey (1985) defined lived experience as those experiences which involve our immediate, pre-reflective consciousness of life.

Outdoor Educational Experiences: A range of experiential activities which take place in outdoor environments (Priest, 1986).

Place-based education: Knapp (2008) described forms of place-based education as "community-based learning, service learning, environment as an integrating concept, environment-based education, outdoor education, bioregional education, ecological education, sustainable-development education, cultural journalism, nature studies, real-world problem-solving, and many others" (p. 6).

Assumptions, Limitations, Delimitations, and Scope

I assumed that the participants in this study would participate willingly and would honestly share their experiences and opinions about their perceptions of their outdoor educational experiences. I assumed that the purposeful sampling strategy and voluntary nature would identify participants who could reflect and articulate their experiences. I assumed that the purposeful sampling strategy would produce results that may be incongruent with other populations. Data collection, analyses, and interpretations for this study were exclusive to the study site.

The boundaries of this study explored outdoor educational experiences based on a single school district's environmental education curriculum. The study site consisted of a rural K–12 school district with approximately 400 students enrolled. This study sought to understand the perceptions of 8 high school seniors in regard to their outdoor educational experiences. The student participants were not categorized by demographic information. Data were collected during the summer of 2010.

The district size and location, the sampling size and method, and the conceptual framework were limitations of this study. One of the limitations of the phenomenological approach was that the findings cannot be generalized (Creswell, 2007, Van Manen, 1990). The study site was a small, rural school with a unique history of a commitment using an outdoor classroom for its environmental education curriculum and was a limitation of this research methodology. The study included the participation of 8 recently graduated high school students. The perceptions of the participants could not be generalized to include the perceptions of other students in the school district or other school districts across the state or other states across the country. Additionally, the participant sample cohort might have exhibited behavioral traits in commons since they shared both a willingness to participate in the interview process and the phenomenon being studied. A phenomenology is a study of perceptions, which are self-reported. Moustakas (1994) stated that a characteristic of phenomenology is that "it is illuminated through careful, comprehensive descriptions, vivid and accurate renderings of the experience, rather than measurements, ratings, or scores" (p.105). Therefore, the hermeneutics of the data were predisposed to various interpretations. The review of the literature found experiential learning theory, sociocultural learning theory, and constructivist theory are the "backbone" of good educational pedagogy and are also integral components of outdoor educational experiences; these theories formed the foundation of the conceptual framework for this study. Throughout the process of analyzing and interpreting the data, I may have held an unintentional bias toward the theories that underpinned the conceptual framework.

Delimitations of this study included the omission of teachers and parents, who could have been important sources of data but were not within the scope of this study. There was no attempt to include perceptions of students outside of the purposefully selected participants of this study. Other outdoor educational experiences offered through the environmental education curriculum of other school districts were not specifically considered.

Significance of the Study

The purpose of this phenomenological study was to explore the essence of meaning in the lived experiences of recently graduated high school students who have taken part in outdoor educational experiences. Kellert (2005) stated that

the decline in children's experience of nature will not change until a fundamental shift occurs in the attitudes and practices of developers, designers, educators, political leaders, and ordinary citizens. The enormous challenge facing us is how to minimize and mitigate the adverse environmental impacts of the modern built environment and how to provide more positive opportunities for contact with nature among children and adults as an integral part of everyday life. (p. 89)

This study explored how students perceive their involvement with outdoor educational experiences.

The findings resulting from this study were applied to the local problem from which this study emanated by providing additional evidence of the importance of outdoor educational experiences so that the school district could make informed decisions on the allocation of funds to best serve student needs. The significance of this study lied in its methodology and analysis of the data to determine students' perceptions and stories as they related to the natural environment as an educational resource. Previous quantitative and qualitative studies on this topic dealt with the impacts of outdoor education, experiential education, and environmentally-based education on environmental knowledge and behaviors, increased academic achievement in other curricular areas, and increased physical and emotional health. This study was important because, while there is abundant literature on the importance of providing students with opportunities to establish a connection with their natural surroundings during environment-based lessons, there is a lack of research that explores students' perceptions of their experiences with outdoor educational experiences. I found no studies documenting student perceptions of the lived experiences as told in the voice of the participants. This study enriched the understanding of the phenomenon and provided educators and others information on the possible value of natural surroundings to young people. This study provided local and state educators with more information related to the investment in and importance of using outdoor classrooms and other natural settings. Positive social change could result from an educational model based on the findings of this research.

Summary of Introduction to the Study

Driven by an increased public perception of children, the No Child Left Inside movement has pushed an environmental education agenda that encouraged educators to incorporate outdoor education throughout the curriculum. This study was inspired by a rural district's desire to effectively utilize an outdoor educational classroom and employed a hermeneutic phenomenological approach to explore the essence of meaning in the lived experiences of recently graduated high school students who participated in outdoor educational experiences. Section 1 included an introduction to the research topic. Section 2 incorporates related literature and current research. Section 3 contains details of the methodology to be used in this study. Section 4 of this study reports the findings of the study. Section 5 concludes this study with interpretations of the findings, related conclusions, the implications for social change, and recommendations for further study.

Section 2: Literature Review

In preparation for conducting this phenomenological study, a review of the professional and research literature was conducted. I began this literature review by searching for research studies concerning the use of outdoor learning environments as an educational resource. Educational theories were explored in an effort to understand if the use of the natural environment within the context of outdoor educational experiences had a firm pedagogical foundation. The third section of this literature review surveyed literature concerning risk factors such as culture and poverty to see if there were links to the use of outdoor environmental activities as a protective factor for students exposed to these risks. Finally, methodological insights were garnered in an effort to support choices made in this study. Using the Academic Search Premier, Educational Resource Information Center (ERIC), Educational Research Complete, PsycARTICLES, and Teacher Reference Center databases, I searched for articles using the following key words and phrases: constructivism, multiple intelligences, achievement gap, place-based education, culturally-relevant, brain-based learning, at-risk youth, experiential learning, academic resilience, learning theory, persistence factor, and intrinsic motivation. The arguments developed in the documents reviewed during this search led me to conclude that many children have become disconnected from their natural environment and that exposure to the natural environment provided benefits for students. I found a lack of studies that explored student perceptions of their outdoor educational experiences and believe that this would be a valuable area of study.

Learning in Outdoor Environments

Learning in an outdoor environment has long been understood to be of value to children. In 1885, Robert Louis Stevenson wrote of this phenomenon in the following verse, "Happy hearts and happy faces, Happy play in grassy spaces, That was how in ancient ages children grew to kings and sages" (Stevenson & Kincaid, 1999, p. 54). Nature-based education uses outdoor settings as a context for delivery of curricular lessons for a variety of pedagogical reasons. Beard and Wilson (2006) stated that "outdoor environments have a long history of providing very special spaces for individuals to learn, in a profound way, about themselves and their social interaction with others" (p.85). Pedagogical constructs using outdoor environments include place-based education, experiential education, and outdoor education.

Place-based Education

The pedagogical construct of place-based education positions learning within the local customs and traditions and within the natural environment. Sobel (2005) defined place-based education as

> the process of using the local community and environment as a starting point to teach concepts in language arts, mathematics, social studies, science, and other subjects across the curriculum. Emphasizing hands-on, real-world learning experiences, this approach to education increases academic achievement, helps students develop ties to their community, enhances students' appreciation for the natural world, and creates a heightened commitment to serving as active, contributing citizens. (p. 7)

Place-based education constructs a holistic and meaningful learning environment by incorporating indigenous culture, nature studies, and authentic tasks based on local community issues. Cole (2007) and Ebersole and Worster (2007) described how place-based pedagogy provided significant learning experiences. Gruenewald (2005) used the local cultural and ecological environments as the basis for educational and community improvement. The chance for students to use authentic learning experiences and an opportunity to develop civic action skills in order to increase educational success was an important aspect of place-based education.

The Rural School and Community Trust (2003) showcased six case studies of programs that established a place-based framework in an effort to engage at–risk youth in a challenging academic program. An example of one of these case studies delineated a program that incorporated a place-based framework in a program located on a Navaho reservation. The problems experienced on the Navaho reservation included a high dropout rate, a high unemployment rate, a high alcoholism rate, and a high depression rate were attributed to a loss of culture, a feeling of subordination, and a lack of a culturally significant education (p. 41). The place-based program incorporated language and culture and provided an educational context that students found relevant. Students and their parents developed pride in their home, in their culture, and in their environment.

Haas and Nachtigal (1998) identified ecology, government, livelihood, spirituality, and community values as issues that need to be addressed if a curriculum is considered place-based. They suggested that educators focus on instilling in students a sense of place, which includes developing sustainable attitudes towards earth's resources, a sense of civic involvement, which includes becoming involved community decision-making, a sense of worth, which includes knowledge of local career opportunities, a sense of connection, which includes an understanding of spirituality or the way a person understands the connections and relationships in their life, and finally, a sense of belonging, which includes a commitment to heritage, cultural values, and history of the community.

Experiential Education

Beard and Wilson (2006) stated that experiential learning is the active engagement of the learner and involves a holistic approach that encompasses the thoughts, feelings, and physical activity. "Experiential learning is the sense-making process of active engagement between the inner world of the person and the outer world of the environment" (p. 2). One of the basic doctrines of experiential learning is making learning personal. Experiential learning is a multifaceted and multilayered with multiple connections with other experiences. Dewey (1916) stated that

> thinking, in other words, is the intentional endeavor to discover specific connections between something which we do and the consequences which result, so that the two become continuous. Their isolation, and consequently, their purely arbitrary going together, is cancelled; a unified, developed situation takes place. (pp. 144 – 145)

Bialeschki (2007) articulated the three Rs of experiential education: relevance, relationships, and real. Relevance revolves around the idea that information needs to be purposeful and meaningful to individual students. Increasing cultural relevance is often discussed as essential to improving education for diverse populations. Relationships refer the network of affiliations students create during experiential opportunities. Cohorts occur amongst the participants and the leadership. The final R is real. Experiential education creates authentic learning opportunities for participants where they can be themselves and be engaged in meaningful activities.

The natural environment becomes the context for students to make the holistic connections to learning. The environment is the classroom. Klug and Whitfield (2003) stated that education among indigenous people was essentially experiential in nature. The children learned by observing their elders. A culturally-relevant curriculum embodies experiential learning. The concepts are taught so that students are able to make the multifaceted, multilayered connections incorporating their worldview and traditional teachings with the learning opportunities in public schools. The critical components of culturally-relevant curriculum included concepts taught within familiar contexts. The emphasis of instruction is incorporated in a holistic picture, rich in relationships and cultural connections. These critical components are essential to experiential education. Barta, et al. (2001) conducted a 2-year qualitative study describing involving semistructured interviews on how a culturally relevant mathematics curriculum. Results indicated an increased need for culturally-relevant curriculum to help American Indian students become more successful in America's Eurocentric educational system.

Outdoor Education

Knapp (1996) identified the main purpose of outdoor education as the provision of meaningful experiences in natural environments in order to complement classroom instruction. Similarly, Broda (2007) stated that schools have used outdoor education to "promote both a knowledge of and a concern for the environment, facilitate personal growth through problem-solving, challenge, and adventure, and focus upon the teaching of traditional subject matter" (p. 6). Rooted in Hahn's philosophy of education, the principles of self-discovery, meeting triumph and defeat, serving a common cause, spending periods of silence, activating the imagination, keeping sports in perspective and creating an equal playing field for all students regardless of their families' wealth and power have become the precepts of outdoor education (Anonymous, 2007). School curricula around the world vary in the use of outdoor education from no use at all to stand alone courses to an infusion of outdoor education into all curricular areas (Bucknell & Mannion, 2006; Davis, Rea, & Waite, 2006). Key concepts of outdoor education also vary according to the level of exposure to natural environments from trip to zoos and museum to natural areas. Research indicated that influences on levels of learning are directly correlated to the increasing levels of wildness (Broda, 2007; Taylor, Kuo, & Sullivan, 2001).

The diversity of experiences referred to as outdoor education make identifying its value as pedagogy difficult to assess. The Forest School in England is a successful educational program that builds on students' inherent motivation and positive attitude toward learning by taking advantage of frequent and regular experiences in the outdoors (Davis & Waite, 2005; Swarbrick, Eastwood & Tutton, 2004). The principles of outdoor education promoted a developmental progression in the successful acquisition of the aesthetic, humanistic, and naturalistic values. In addition, nature played a role in the affective and cognitive development of children. To ensure continued success of the program, recommendations include the constant review of the principles and pedagogy reflects the goals of the school.

Outdoor education places an emphasis on both interpersonal and intrapersonal skills (Hill, 2007; Priest & Gass, 1997; Zink & Burrows, 2006). Building upon the ideals of experiential education, outdoor education programs augment independent, participatory learning. Effective outdoor education programs are built upon a holistic approach (Adams & Sveen, 2000; Hubball & West, 2009). The development of holistic learning focused on the physical, mental, social, emotional, spiritual, and environmental components of a healthy self-esteem (Green & Kreuter, 2005; Sheinfeld-Gorin & Arnold, 2006). Spiritual well-being is a critical component of holistic learning as it provides the learner with a sense of meaning in relation to a personal worldview during times of reflection. Spiritual well-being can be enhanced when students are encouraged to explore feelings during educational programs (Adams & Sveen, 2000; Chawla, 1999; Hall, 2007; Uhlik, 2009).

Educational Theories

Experiential Learning Theory

Dewey (1938) was the founder of the philosophical school of pragmatism. He believed that school was one of the key areas that needed attention in order to improve society and he believed that learning best happened in a realm in which communication, the sharing of an experience until it became a common possession, was the basis of effective education. Dewey promoted the idea that teachers should not deliver knowledge but should provide experiences upon which students can build understanding. Dewey advocated the idea that if teachers used hands-on methods that provided opportunities for practical problem solving, learning would be increased. Dewey summarized his thoughts on education:

I have taken for granted the soundness of the principle that education in order to accomplish its ends both for the individual learner and for society must be based on experience which is always the actual life-experience of some individual. (p.89)

Experience is the teacher; educators provide opportunities for students to experience.

Freire (2008) built upon Deweyan paradigms of building learning on experiences. Freire discussed how students need to become a part of their learning rather than a receptacle of information. Freire's two types of knowledge included an unconscious or practical knowledge and a critical or reflective knowledge. Students exposed to a situation build their understanding of the situation through discussion and reflection. "Only dialogue, which requires critical thinking, is also capable of generating critical thinking. Without dialogue there is no communication, and without communication there can be no true education" (pp. 92-93). Students need to build or construct knowledge based upon previous knowledge in order to learn. Schein (2003) discussed the role of dialogue in communication failures and cultural misunderstandings. Schein contended that all people are culturally trained to maintain social order and we are taught from a young age to claim a certain amount of status for ourselves when we communicate to others. Schein stressed the importance of continued dialogue to affect learning across cultural boundaries.

Sociocultural Theory

The importance of communication in learning is also an integral part of Vygotsky's (1956) sociocultural theory. According to Vygotsky's theory, children gained their existing knowledge and their learning style through their culture. Children increase their cognitive skills by working cooperatively in problem-solving experiences. Vygotsky believed that culture was crucial to a child's intellectual development.

Sociocultural theory is characterized by an emergent view of human development that is dependent upon social interactions. Vygotsky argued that children's learning is a function of the child's interactions with his/her environment. When viewed through a sociocultural lens, the teaching and learning environment takes on a holistic aspect in which the context where instruction occurs is interwoven with content pedagogy and actions of teaching behaviors. The bounds of Vygotsky's zone of proximal development were between what children learn on their own and what they can learn with the help others. The theory of cooperative learning is supported by Vygotsky's zone of proximal development and stressed positive, face-to-face, small group interactions with individual and group accountability (Doolittle, 1995).

Naturalist Intelligence Theory

Gardner promoted the idea that instead of a singular intelligence, humans exhibit several intelligences. Gardner identified linguistic, logical-mathematical, musical, spatial, bodily-kinesthetic, interpersonal, intrapersonal, and naturalistic intelligences (Moran, Kornhaber, & Gardner, 2006). Gardner pointed out that human beings are a complex, interacting group of intelligences with one or more intelligences dominant to others. Rooted in Gardner's naturalistic intelligence work, Louv's (2005) nature-deficit disorder was identified as a condition resulting from isolation from the natural environment. Louv explored how the lack of exposure to nature negatively influenced the ability of people to learn.

Sternberg's (1990) theory of intelligence juxtaposed Gardner's theory of multiple intelligences. Gardner (2005) alleged that the expression of the intelligences was biologically determined and their expression was shaped and socialized by culture. Sternberg believed that intelligence is acquired rather than biologically predetermined. Sternberg stressed that culture must be taken into account because cultural values shape the expression of intelligence (Messick, 1992).

Implicit knowledge is an important concept for the school setting. Sternberg speculated that a student without implicit knowledge from of cultural training would not have the declarative and procedural knowledge necessary for academic success. The Yale Practical Intelligence for School program combined the instruction based on Gardner and Sternberg in order to develop declarative and procedural knowledge. This program was based on teaching students to become independent learners who are able to manage themselves and their tasks and are able to work as a contributing member of a team (Sternberg, Okagaki, & Jackson, 1990).

Brain-based Learning

Brain-based learning is based on the neurological structure and function. The brain continuously searches for meaning as it processes sensory information from its surroundings. The brain is most effective at learning when a person is immersed in a personally challenging situation. Human cognition is improved when the learning opportunity provides opportunities to reflect and process the information that was gathered during the activity. "Throughout life, the brain constantly 'reconstructs' itself in order to cope with on-going changes, and meet the ever-changing demands, the cognitive, behavioral and emotional status of an organism is remodeled by this lifelong self-adjustment and self-optimization processes" (Gulpinar, 2005, p. 300). Creating an emotional and social climate for learning, creating rich, complex and realistic experiences with opportunities to reflect, find, and construct meaningful connections and creating ways to consolidate learning by constructing mental models. These principles merge seamlessly with the theory of constructivist learning.

Constructivist Theory

Constructivist learning theory is supported by the concept that students use existing knowledge to construct revised theories of the world. Proponents of constructivist learning describe the need for educational opportunities that rich with experiential opportunities and opportunities to practice critical thinking in order to facilitate students' ability to build new understandings.

Situated and contextualized learning provides dynamic connections between culturally-relevant instruction and constructivism. This learning permits the student to transfer existing knowledge to new constructs of real-life situations (Hankes, 1991; Nelson-Barber & Estrin, 1995). Learning takes place when students are in charge of their acquisition of knowledge in a culturally-rich environment that provides time for reflection (Hankes, 1991, p. 3). Collaborative problem-solving with opportunities for reflection is an important piece of a constructivist classroom.

Academic Risk Factors

Poverty

The Annie E. Casey Foundation Data Book (2009) analyzed compiled data on child well-being based on health, adequacy of income, and educational attainment from birth to early adulthood. According to these data, 33% of American Indian/Alaskan

Native children live in poverty. In addition, American Indian/Alaskan Native adolescents and Hispanic/Latino adolescents have disproportionate dropout rates when compared to the national average for all adolescents. Prince, Pepper, and Brocato (2006) found a direct relationship between family income and academic achievement. Outcomes of poverty such as poor nutrition, lack of access to health care, and low birth weight are predictors of low achievement rates in school.

Poverty can be short-term and situational or it can be generational, which is defined as a family living in poverty for successive generations (Payne, 1996). The effects of generational poverty are insidious and can be felt even when individuals who grew up in poverty experience an increase in income. In fact, living in poverty is characterized not only by income, but also by the lack of emotional, mental, spiritual, physical, support systems, and role model resources. The hidden rules of class structure such as not having a sufficient vocabulary to communicate with those in a higher class because of lack of education, lack of social mannerisms, and lack of understandings of the underlying values of a different social stratum can trap children in the cycle of poverty.

Minority Status

Racial disproportionality in student achievement is an important aspect of school reform. Researchers (Chen & Weikart, 2008; Fram, Miller-Cribbs, & Van Horn, 2007; Marks & Coll, 2007; McGee, 2004) have studied issues of race. Fram, et al., 2007, found that children with single parents and children attending high minority schools tended to have more difficulties achieving success in school. The subsets of participants included in this study were White, Black, and Hispanic public school students in the southern United

States. The variables analyzed in this study included reading skills, classroom variables, child and family variables, and school variables. While several factors--including a less experienced teaching staff and less adequately equipped classrooms may have influenced the findings from this study, it was found that White students living in poverty conditions followed the same patterns of low achievement as did students of color.

Chen and Weikart (2008) studied the correlation between school disorder and student achievement in an effort to determine the impact of risk factors on student achievement. The data set for this empirical study stemmed from 212 middle schools in New York City. The data set was selected because of the increased influence of school climate on this age group. It is at this level that students experienced an increase in violence and crime. An analysis of the data supported the hypothesis that poverty and minority status predicted school disorder and school disorder directly correlated to lower achievement levels. The data also supported a conclusion that higher level of poverty produced a decrease in student attendance.

The Golden Spike schools in Illinois have documented a sustained closing of the achievement gap. McGee (2004) studied the difference in the performance of students that were low-income and/or a minority with students who were members of a more advantaged population. McGee used both qualitative and quantitative methodologies to determine that literacy, leadership, teacher qualities and community engagement played a larger role in student achievement than did class size, school size, or an alignment with state standards.

Results from a study of the development of early academic skills of American Indian students found that poverty and parent education had a significant impact (Marks

& Coll, 2007). Data for this study were obtained from generated by 22,000 kindergartners from throughout the United States. A preliminary analysis was conducted using descriptive statistics and Pearson correlations and was followed by latent growth modeling. Additional studies documented issues related to American Indian academic achievement. For example, Pewewardy (2002) provided an example of the way that culture is used by non-Indian people in an idiom known as *Indian time*. When an American Indian student is late for school, it is blamed on *Indian time* when it may have been because of helping a single working mother with the care of younger siblings. Similarly, *Indian time* may be blamed when a tribal member fails to get to a meeting on time, when the real reason may have been because the car broke down. Both of these events are commonly linked to poverty but are mistakenly attributed to cultural traditions.

Ogbu (2004) defined collective identity as "people's sense of who they are, their 'we-feeling' or 'belonging.' People expressed their collective identity with emblems or cultural symbol which reflect their attitudes, beliefs, feelings, behaviors, and language or dialect" (p. 3). Minorities find status problems such as

1) Involuntary incorporation into society because minorities do not usually become minorities by choice;

2) Instrumental discrimination such as denial of access to good jobs, education, political participation, and housing,

3) Social subordination, which includes residential and social segregation, and,

4) Expressive mistreatment: for example, cultural, language, and intellectual denigration (p. 4).

Ogbu recommended that minority students recognize that these factors exist and suggested that minority students focus less on status problems and more on their response to the status problems.

Gibson (2005) and Foley (2005) discussed Ogbu's theory in an analysis and critique and found that he failed to consider school intercessions promoting school engagement.

> Creating a sense of belonging or membership in the school community may be especially important for minority students, due both to the power differential that exists between themselves and members of the dominant society and due to the discontinuities that many minority students experience between home and school cultures. (Gibson, p. 596)

The responsibility for building relationships between the teachers and the students and building supportive peer relationships needs to be a primary function of schools. Gibson stated that schools need to help students build social capital and instructional support to help students increase their career aspirations.

Lew (2006) extended the Ogbu's theory of 'acting white' to racial groups other than Blacks. Lew's studies used high and low achieving student participants. First and second generation Korean American students were included in the study. Lew's case studies supported the findings of Gibson when she argued that race, class, and school context are important elements in the academic success of Asian students. She found that middle-class, high-achievement Korean American students felt that they could use education as a strategy to achieve economic parity with the white Americans even though they felt that they would have to work harder to achieve the same levels of success.

Korean high school dropouts adapted by aligning themselves with other minority students.

Studies (Goldsmith, 2004; Tyson, 2002) demonstrated a causal link in a longitudinal study of a stratified-random sample of 24,599 eighth grade students who were of mixed race and ethnicity that indicated that schools that employed minority teachers generated an increase in students' occupational expectations, aspirations, and attitudes(Goldsmith, 2004). The quantitative study used survey data from students, parents, teachers, and school principals. Tyson (2002) conducted a study at two all-black high schools in the southeastern United States in which 56 students were interviewed and observations of their classrooms were conducted. The schools in this study came from a diversity of geographic and socioeconomic areas. Tyson found that several factors including class, peer networks, and school context influenced academic success.

Native American Education

American Indian students are faced with many stressors that put them at-risk of not being academically successful. The philosophies and culture of American Indian students are centered in a sense of place (Barnhardt, 2008; Connell-Szasz, 1974/1999; Deloria & Wildcat, 2001; Fixico, 2003; Reyhner & Eder, 2004). A sense of place incorporates nature studies, cultural studies, and authentic problem solving. Educators may increase academic resilience in American Indian students through the provision of a culturally-relevant, rigorous curriculum based on the concepts of place-based education. The connection of the American Indian with nature and the workings of the Indian mind are intimately connected spiritually and intellectually (Fixico, 2003, p. xii). Balance is an important part of the American Indian philosophy. "At least five kinds of balance exist:

(1) balance within one's self, (2) balance within the family, (3) balance within the community or tribe, (4) balance with external communities, including other tribes and the spiritual world, and (5) balance with the environment and the universe" (Fixico, 2003, p. 49). The Eurocentric perception of humanity is that humans are the center of activity. In contrast, Indian people perceive themselves to be a small part of a larger whole and recognize the natural world as an equal party to be mutually respected.

Bowman (2003) analyzed American Indian populations in Wisconsin and found data which supported the disparity between the achievement levels of White students and American Indian students. This study found that the disparity was greater in both the areas of graduation rates and enrollment in post-secondary institutions and was greater than any other minority group. The differences between a Eurocentric worldview and an American Indian worldview influenced the ability of the American Indian student to achieve academic success. Bowman found that school curricula needed to incorporate American Indian history, culture, and language in order to help American Indian students close the academic achievement gap. Additional studies discussed additional factors that impacted the ability of the American Indian student to be academically successful. These include differences in learning styles, a lack of student motivation, a low socioeconomic status, a lack of trust in government-run schools, and a lack of understanding of cultural differences (Beaulieu, 2000; Leveque, 1994).

A gap in academic scores of Native American students could, to a certain extent, be attributed to the influences of culture and environment (Demmert, 2006, p. 16). An American Indian student stated,

In school I felt really isolated and really alienated and really alone. The Indian

way of behaving is: you watch and you observe before you act. You don't want to

make a fool out of yourself in front of the group because of the shame culture.

You observe, and so once you know what's expected of you, then you act, but you

never want to show off because it's not good taste to pound your own drum.

(Education, 2004, p. 34)

A lack of respect for the culture and language led this student to a feeling of alienation

from teachers and peers.

Connell-Szasz (2003) discussed the use of boarding schools to prepare American

Indian students for assimilation into mainstream culture. The United States government

had used American Indian boarding schools to indoctrinate Indian children into White

culture through the process of enculturation in order to make the American Indian more

like the white man (Connell-Szasz, 2003). A residual disquiet continues to permeate

subsequent generations of American Indian students including students who are currently

attending public schools. This distrust creates an obstacle to implementing a successful

curriculum. This cultural distrust sets up an innate contradiction "since 'culture' (Ojibwe)

is distinguished from 'academics,' academic success is associated with Whiteness and is

tantamount to assimilation" (Hermes, 2000, p. 389). Hermes also discussed American

Indian's conviction that a choice between "being smart" and "being Indian" must be

made. In order for American Indian students to find academic success, the belief that

success equals a rejection of cultural identity has to be effectively eradicated.

American Indian children are brought up in a culturally different environment

until they first go to public school. McInerney & McInerney (2000) stated, "It is essential for teachers to have knowledge of, recognize, come to understand, and accommodate within the regular school programs the value systems characterizing these children which reflect their sociocultural backgrounds" (p. 3). The findings of a 3-year study found that American Indian students were motivated to attend school because of punitive consequences rather than by future goals. American Indian students described increased peer pressure to engage in negative behaviors involving drugs and alcohol as a reason for their lack of success at school. They also identified dysfunctional family backgrounds as an inhibitor more frequently than the White population did. American Indian students reported a greater difficulty because of a lack of cultural relevance in school and did not link a college education with their future needs. Both White and American Indian students emphasized the importance of parental/family interest as the foremost motivator for school achievement (McInerney & McInerney, 2000, p. 8-9).

Sparks (2000) endorsed the importance of teachers needing to be instructed on specific tribal cultures of the American Indian students they teach in order to meet the learning of these students. When working with American Indian students, Sparks recommended that teachers avoid overgeneralization and focus on oral tradition, colorful visual aids, real life examples, and experiential learning techniques and avoid stereotypes.

Nelson, Simonsen, & Swanson (2003) stated, "the Native American culture is holistic, integrating the community, the individual, the environment, and spirituality. In traditional Native American communities, what is good for an individual is inextricably linked to the good of the entire community" (p. 9). This working paper recommended an "instructional sequence for Native American students based a constructivist approach to learning with a sociocultural perspective, which will encourage instructors to teach concepts in meaningful contexts through the processes of inquiry and exploration that reinforce the value of Native American culture" (p. 17). An experiential approach along with a constructivist methodology was found to be successful in helping American Indian students close the achievement gap.

Starnes (2006) stated, "First, most Native children learn best when hands-on, experiential teaching and learning approaches are used. Second, there is a positive relationship between students' academic learning and their strong sense of cultural identity. And third, informal and flexible learning environments enhance native students' learning" (p. 387). Understanding the modalities of learning based on "Indian thinking" provides a richer learning environment for American Indian students and is supported by outdoor educational experiences.

The College Board's National Task Force on Minority High Achievement investigated the issue of low proportions of minority students found in the high achievement category of all levels of academics. The College Board suggested, "the notion that our nation has both a strong moral and practical interest in taking an extensive array of public and private actions designed to ensure that underrepresented minority groups significantly increase their rate of educational progress" (College Board, 1999, p. 3). McCombs (2000) delineated "research-validated learner-centered principles which create positive learning environments that aid in increased achievement for underachieving African American, Latino, and American Indian groups" (p. 32). In order to close the achievement gap, McCombs concluded that "what must change are the cultures of schools as well as the curriculum, such that the knowledge systems, ideologies, perspectives, and behaviors of diverse ethnic, racial, cultural, social class and language groups are institutionalized and legitimized" (p. 35). Outdoor educational experiences may provide an opportunity for improved learning by recognizing the various learning modalities found in diverse cultures.

Academic Resilience

The National Research Council (2003) stated that obstacles to the successful education of American youth may include risk factors such as living in a family with a low socioeconomic status, emotional and behavioral disabilities, cultural influences, poor attendance and a lack of motivation. Students' "failure to acquire the basic skills needed to function in adult society, whether or not they complete high school, dramatically increases their risks of unemployment, poverty, poor health, and involvement in the criminal justice system" (p. 211). To understand how to address the aforementioned obstacles, it may be helpful to look at why students experiencing the same risk factors are successful. Morales (2008b) defined academic resilience as "the phenomenon of statistically unlikely academic achievement among marginalized and disenfranchised students" (p. 23). An educational system such as a school district has little power to ameliorate risk factors such as poverty; they do have the resources necessary to help students increase academic resilience.

There are many risk factors that can inhibit a child's normal development. The concept of resilience has been frequently studied in recent literature; however, little is understood about why one student will exhibit resilience while another impacted by the same risk factors is not. Martin, as cited in Smith (2006), stated, "psychology is not just the study of weakness and damage; it is also the study of strength and virtue. Treatment is not just fixing what is broken; it is nurturing what is best within ourselves" (p. 13).

While it is helpful to understand what factors have been identified as risk factors, learning about the factors that can promote resilience may be more effective in helping students achieve success.

A "misconception is that the findings from resilience research only apply to 'high-risk youth'" (Benard, p. 9). All students are exposed to some type of risk factors at some point in their school careers. Resilience studies have identified four personal strengths that provide the skills necessary to cope with risk factors whether they are impacting a high-risk population or a low-risk student caught up in a stressful situation. Werner and Smith (1992) discussed how "the buffers (protective factors) make a more profound impact on the life course of children who grow up under adverse conditions than do specific risk factors or stressful life events. They appear to transcend ethnic, social class, geographical, and historical boundaries" (p. 202). According to Benard (2004) the personal strengths that provide high resilience for dealing with risk factors include social competence, problem-solving, autonomy, and a sense of purpose.

There are many studies (Black & Lobo, 2008; Gordon, 1995; Morales, 2008a) that have looked at resilience factors and found that self-concept, motivation, conscientiousness, independence, social skills, and an internal locus of control are key factors leading to academic resilience. Nurturing these strengths may provide an increase in resilience to students. Garmezy (1991) stressed the importance of schools in providing the critical support system for children struggling for success in dealing with many of the risk factors. "Teachers, peers, and curricula all play important roles in the growing child's development" (p. 425). Garmezy included high expectations, out-of-school activities, academic and work-oriented goals, and maintenance of a prosocial atmosphere as ways that schools can help nurture resilience in students.

Exposure to natural environments might be a protective factor contributing to the unanticipated academic success of youth. Louv (2008) stated that "nature is often overlooked as a healing balm for the emotional hardships in a child's life" (p. 49). Louv identified nature-deficit disorder as a sickness resulting from a human estrangement from nature. Louv provided examples of how the lack of exposure yielded a "diminished use of the senses, attention difficulties, and higher rates of physical and emotional illnesses, while an enriched exposure to nature can influence the ability of children to learn biologically, cognitively, and spiritually" (Louv, 2008, p. 36). Wilson (1984) identified the human attraction to nature as *biophilia*. Wilson's theory of biophilia stated that the human bond with nature is rooted in our biology; that it is through this bond that humans refine their experience and culture. When stories of experiences with the natural world are shared, cultural, political, and religious barriers are overcome. Wilson (1998) discussed the concepts of holism in the belief that all knowledge is interwoven, that "we are drowning in information, while starving for wisdom. The world henceforth was run by synthesizers, people able to put together the right information at the right time, think critically about it, and make important choices wisely" (p. 294). Qualitative studies (Ernst & Monroe, 2006, Cachelin, et al., 2009) have demonstrated that using environment-based education as a source of real world learning experiences increased students' critical thinking skills. While the current literature has contributed to the study of academic resilience and the importance of outdoor experiences, the research has not considered the relationship between academic resilience and exposure to the natural environment.

Children benefit from exposure to natural environments; however, direct contact with nature is becoming a rare experience for many children. Kellert stated, "...play in nature, particularly during the critical period of middle childhood, appears to be an especially important time for developing the capacities for creativity, problem-solving, and emotional and intellectual development" (p. 83). In addition, Burdette & Whitaker (2005) reinforced these cognitive benefits while emphasizing the health benefits of unstructured free play. Health benefits include fighting childhood obesity while social benefits of unstructured play included building social skills, reducing stress, and reducing aggression. Social benefits of exposure to natural environments are amplified when familial mentors are part of the process, increasing the benefits to both child and parent or other family member (Chawla, 2007; Lester & Maudsley, 2006). Creativity, self-efficacy, and confidence, in addition to the increase in environmental literacy, are all listed as benefits of interaction with natural environments. Cobb (1977) found that the effects of outdoor educational experiences was " a major clue to mental and psychosocial, as well as psychophysical, health lies in the spontaneous and innately creative imagination of childhood" (p. 15).

A study by Faber Taylor, Kuo, & Sullivan (2002) found that attention deficit symptoms were ameliorated after a child spent time in a natural setting. In addition, the more time the child spent in a natural setting, the more manageable the symptoms were. The population for this quantitative study consisted of 452 parents and guardians recruited through websites and ads in major American newspapers. Participants completed an on-line questionnaire made up of 49 survey questions in which parents and guardians could rate activities, physical settings, and social contexts that their children experienced outside of school. In a quantitative study of 337 rural children in grades three through five, Wells & Evans (2003) used the Lewis Stressful Life Events Scale, the Rutter Child Behavior Questionnaire, and the Global Self-Worth subscale of the Harter Competency scale to collect data that support the hypothesis that even a view of nature helped reduce stress in children and increased their ability to focus.

Within an ecological system, diversity provides a layer of protection against stress factors. In an educational system based on the standards and accountability requisites of the No Child Left Behind legislation, schools become a monoculture with a focus on memorization of facts to score well on high stakes tests rather than on developing an understanding of the concepts. Holt (2005) likened this to a fast food restaurant. Meat on a bun might satisfy your immediate hunger, but it does little to meet your nutritional needs and little to nourish your soul. Holt recommends the development of slow schools where the goal is to develop the intellect of students rather than fast schools where government-mandated accountability drives education. Holt declared that "in an age when the right of adults to shape their lifestyle is taken for granted, the right of children to an education that will help them make something of themselves is more circumscribed than ever" (p.57). The incorporation of outdoor-based activities may provide the diversity needed to meet the educational needs of our children.

Methodological Insights

The results from The American Institute for Research (2005) study on the effects of outdoor education programs demonstrated positive outcomes regarding the benefits of outdoor learning experiences for at-risk students. The population for this study consisted of sixth-grade students from geographically diverse schools. The treatment group attended an outdoor education program three times in a 3-month period. The control group had not attended the outdoor education program but would be attending after the study. This ensured no student would be denied the possible benefits of the experience while providing the researchers with a rigorous methodology for identifying the outcomes of the program. The American Institute for Research (AIR) study used a mixed method approach consisting of surveys and site visits. Among the recommendations for further research, AIR suggested the benefits of further research including a longitudinal study to determine the impacts of outdoor education programs. This study determined the long-term impacts of outdoor education programs but explored the impact these experiences from the perspectives of recent high school graduates who were involved in outdoor education programs. The AIR study focused on personal and social skills, students' environmental stewardship and knowledge of science concepts. This study focused on the perceptions of recent high school graduates rather than focusing on the quantitative strategies of treatment effect using pretest, post test, and delayed surveys.

Matsuoka (2008) revealed that students' academic achievement benefited from exposure to nature even if that exposure was through a window. The purpose of Matsouka's study was to gain an increased understanding of how the design of the school structure and the school's landscaping affected students. A quantitative methodology was appropriate for this cause and effect study. This study analyzed data from public schools; all of the data were from existing data sets. Matsuoka used data from high schools because there was existing research on elementary and middle school levels.

Based on similar reasoning, the participants for this study are recent high school graduates. In the Matsouka study, the results were statistically relevant and supported the study's hypotheses. However, they did not provide the robust answers to why and how exposure to nature benefited students. This study sought the perceptions of students' understandings of their experiences with outdoor education. An exploration of the whys and how's of an experience are indicative of a qualitative methodology.

Blair (2009) conducted an examination of the evaluative literature on school garden outcomes and found quantitative studies that supported the hypotheses that school yard gardening improved science scores and food behaviors but failed to support the hypotheses that school yard gardening changed environmental attitudes or social behavior. Blair reported qualitative studies that provided a wider scope of understanding school yard gardening outcomes on positive social and environmental behaviors. Among the suggestions for further research, Blair discussed the need for quantitative studies without methodological shortcomings to strengthen confidence in the results. In addition, the reviewed studies, both quantitative and qualitative targeted elementary students, teachers, and curriculum indicating a need for this study to understand the continuing effects of these outdoor educational experiences on students who are successfully completing their secondary education.

The Athman and Monroe study (2004a) looked at the relationship between environment-based education and high school students' motivation to succeed. Results supported the hypothesis that environment-based education is related to positive student motivation to succeed. The mixed-method study used a pretest, post test nonequivalent comparison group design with freshmen high school students, and a post test only nonequivalent comparison group design with senior high school students. Participants in this study included students from Florida schools and were selected through operational construct sampling and maximum variation sampling. Participants were enrolled in environment-based education programming for at least two years and represented a range of student socioeconomic statuses, geographic locations, and achievement levels providing external validity to the study. The quantitative portion of this study utilized a survey while the qualitative portion was used to find out what teachers and students believed influenced motivation. Both teachers and students were interviewed with data gathered through audiotapes and field notes. Qualitative data used inductive analysis to find themes. Frequency and extensiveness of responses were also considered. Recommendations for further study included exploring the connection between the natural environment and student motivation and the relationship among motivation, environment-based education, and ethnicity.

This study is heavily influenced by these recommendations although it is focused on how students describe and understand the essence of their experiences with outdoor educational experiences. Outdoor educational experiences are often part of environment-based education but include all lessons conducted outdoors whether the school curriculum is traditional or environment-based. This study will use a similar analytical method in which data are clustered into similar themes.

Hermeneutic Phenomenology

Laverty (2003) discussed the historical antecedents of phenomenology, which was based on the works of Husserl (1959 – 1938) and compared them to the precepts of hermeneutic phenomenology. According to Laverty, Husserl believed that psychology dealt with "living subjects who are not simply reacting automatically to external stimuli, but rather are responding to their own perception of what these stimuli mean" (p. 4). Phenomenology is a search for the meaning of several individuals' description of the phenomenon's essence. Van Manen (1990) defined essence as "that what makes a thing what it is (and without which it would not be what it is); that what makes a thing what it is rather than its being or becoming something else" (p. 177). The essence of the experience is the holistic understanding of the experience.

Husserl (1970) focused phenomenological research on the understanding of the phenomenon. Laverty (2003) explained how Heidegger (1889 – 1976) diverged from Husserl's teachings into hermeneutic phenomenological, which emphasized the "view of people and the world as indissolubly related in cultural, in social, and in historical contexts" (p. 8). A participant's understanding of a phenomenon is seen through the lens of their background, their culture and their other life influences that make up their worldview. Hermeneutic phenomenological research treats the human experience as a semantic and textual structure as the researcher attempts to explore a full account of a particular phenomenon rather than an accurate analysis of the participants' description.

Gadamer (1998) moved beyond Heidegger's work into practical application of hermeneutic phenomenology. Gadamer described hermeneutics as mediation between assumptions and a genuine understanding, with ontology instead of epistemology. "Understanding is always more than merely re-creating someone else's meaning. Questioning opens up possibilities of meaning, and thus what is meaningful passes into one's own thinking on the subject" (p. 375). Understanding and interpretation of an experience is a continuously evolving process.

Van Manen (1990) discussed the interplay of six research activities in the pursuit of hermeneutic phenomenological research. The first of these activities includes finding a phenomenon of interest to study. The second involves investigating the phenomenon as it is lived not as it is imagined. The third research activity involves reflecting on the essential themes characterizing the phenomenon. The fourth activity describes the phenomenon through the iterative writing process in order to maintain a pedagogical relationship to the phenomenon. The final activity describes the balancing of the research context by considering the parts and the whole (p. 31). The resulting phenomenological description is but a single view of the phenomenon, other interpretations are always possible. Like a prism, viewing the phenomenological data from slightly different viewpoints changes the viewer's perceptions.

Summary of Literature Review

The conceptual framework guiding this study was rooted in the lived experiences of participants. The framework was supported by Sobel's (2005) principles of place-based education, Beard & Wilson's (2006) doctrine of experiential education, and Hahn's axiom of outdoor education. The conceptual framework was also supported by the theoretical foundations developed by Dewey (1938), Freire (2008), Schein (2003), Vygotsky (1986), Gardner (2005), Sternberg (1990), Gulpinar (2005), and Hankes (1991). The premise that participation in outdoor educational experiences may be beneficial to students seemed to be supported by the literature but I found a lack of research on understanding the lived experiences of purposefully selected participants who experienced outdoor education. The ideas bounded by the conceptual framework were explored through the voices of participants who experienced learning through outdoor

educational experiences using the methodology discussed in Section Three.

Section 3: Research Method

In this hermeneutic phenomenological study, I examined the lived experiences of participants who engaged in outdoor educational activities presented as part of their district's elementary environmental education curriculum. According to Van Manen (1990), hermeneutic phenomenology is concerned with developing a sophisticated understanding of an experience through the examination of the essence of the experiential meanings as lived in everyday existence. In this section, I detail the hermeneutic phenomenological research design and the plans for data collection and analysis for this research study. I described the setting and population, my role as the researcher, and ethical considerations.

The purpose of this study was to understand the essence of the lived experiences of recently graduated high school students who took part in outdoor educational experiences. As I searched for the best methodology to fulfill this purpose, I considered both quantitative and qualitative methods. Understanding the essence of human experience is not easily accomplished through quantitative studies which, according to Creswell (2003), are an attempt to quantify the impact of a phenomenon. Qualitative research attempts to understand the "hows and whys" of the phenomenon. I chose qualitative research in order to provide a holistic focus on an experience (Moustakas, 1994).

The constructivist paradigm guided my decision to use qualitative research. Hatch (2002) described the constructivist paradigm as being distinguished by an ontology in which universal realities are unknowable and where multiple realities can be constructed based on individual vantage points. The epistemology of the constructivist paradigm is based on researcher and participant constructing knowledge together. The methodology of the constructivist paradigm requires researchers to spend extended periods of time interviewing participants in natural settings to make sense of the participants' world. Qualitative research pursues an understanding of the research issue from the participant's perspective. It is the essence of the experience from the perspective of the participant that provides the rich qualitative data from which understanding can be explicated.

Qualitative research was founded on the idea that researchers collect descriptive data to determine interpretations, grounded in the data, through inductive analysis (Creswell, 2007). The intent of this research was to search for answers about human behaviors in a holistic manner. Methodologically, the theoretical perspective used in the development of this study was based on the interpretivist nature of phenomenology. In this perspective, the goal was to understand the experience from the participant's point of view. Edmund Husserl, a founder of the phenomenological perspective, believed that people "can know only what they experience. They interpret what they experience to the point that descriptions and interpretations of experience are intertwined. There was no objective reality for people. Subjective experience incorporates the objective experience and the individual's interpretation" (as cited in Wanat, 2006, p. 3). There are many possible interpretations of the data depending on the theoretical framework.

Keeping the purpose of this study at the forefront of the decision making process, several qualitative methodological strategies were considered but rejected for this study. Ethnography was considered but rejected for this study because its focus is on intact cultures and the aim of this study is to understand the stories of individuals. Narrative research was considered but rejected for this study because its focus is the exploration of the life of an individual. Grounded theory research was considered but rejected for this study because its focus is on a process, or interaction. Case study was given a great deal of consideration but rejected for this study because case studies are concerned with an in-depth understanding of an event, program, or activity--not the interpretation of the lived experiences of several individuals who have experienced a phenomenon. Van Manen (1990) stated "from a phenomenological point of view, we are less interested in the factual status of particular interests: whether something actually happened, how often it tends to happen, or how the occurrence of an experience is related to the prevalence of other conditions or events" (p. 10). The purpose of phenomenology is not to reduce the phenomenon into clearly defined concepts but to bring an increased depth of understanding to the phenomenon.

Using the phenomenological perspective, I probed the participants' realities as they interpreted them. Participants recalled an experience based on their individual worldviews. Lived experiences provided concrete insights into the unique meanings of a phenomenon for the individual. I searched for commonalities among multiple participants' experiences to determine the shared fundamental nature of the phenomenon. Participants' experiences were analyzed through Blumer's (1986) symbolic interactionism framework, which helped me to view social dialogue as a product of interactions. The findings were analyzed through the lens of symbolic interactionism. Symbolic interactionism was originated in the work of Blumer (1986), who described it as a way to determine the meanings of social dialogue as products or creations formed in and through the interactions of people. Wanat (2006) stated that "people create shared meanings through interactions and act according to how they see their world, not according to external rules or norms. Shared meanings become reality" (p. 3). Interviewing student participants and probing their interpretations of their lived experience helped me understand the phenomenon.

Researchers may be predisposed or biased in their interpretations so they need to bracket out their own experiences to approach the interview with an "unbiased, receptive presence" (Moustakas, 1994, p. 180). Van Manen (1990) discussed explicating assumptions and pre-understandings. "The problem is that our 'common sense' pre-understandings, our suppositions, assumptions, and the existing bodies of scientific knowledge, predispose us to interpret the nature of the phenomenon before we have come to grips with the significance of the problem" (p. 47). Bracketing allowed me to "come to terms with [my] assumptions, not in order to forget them again, but rather to hold them deliberately at bay and even to turn this knowledge against itself, as it were, thereby exposing its shallow or concealing character" (Van Manen, 1990, p. 47). Acknowledging predispositions allows the researcher to focus on the significance of the lived experiences of the participants as they relate to the phenomenological question being studied.

In hermeneutic phenomenology, the researcher must be constantly mindful of the phenomenological question. Creswell (2007) suggested that the researcher focus the study by asking participants two questions: "What have you experienced in terms of the phenomenon? What contexts or situations have typically influenced or affected your experiences of the phenomenon?" (p. 61). The question(s) must interrogate something from the core of the phenomenon in an attempt to reveal its essence. Van Manen (1990) recommended that the phenomenological question address what the experience is really like. The phenomenological question(s) must allow the researcher to remain open to all possibilities.

The goal of hermeneutic phenomenology is not to reduce the phenomenon into clearly defined concepts, but rather to bring about a comprehensive understanding of the phenomenological experience. The emphasis of this type of research is to use other people's experiences to better understand the deeper meaning of the phenomenon in the holistic context of the human experience. Van Manen (1990) stated that participant stories of their experience with the phenomenon allow the researcher to become more experienced with the phenomenon themselves (p. 62). The semistructured interview serves as a means to gather lived-experience material. The interview becomes increasingly hermeneutic as the researcher uses the occasion to allow the participant to reflect on the experience. Van Manen continued with a recommendation to remember that

> it is important to realize that it is not of great concern whether a certain experience actually happened in exactly that way. We are less concerned with the factual accuracy of an account than with the plausibility of an account – whether it is true to our living sense of it. (p. 65)

Participants begin to interpret their understandings of their lived experiences as soon as they happen. Hermeneutic phenomenology is interested in the essence of the lived experience, which is based upon the current description provided by the participant rather than an accurate play-by-play of the experience.

Organization and analysis of the data in a hermeneutical phenomenology begins when frames of analysis are identified from the transcribed interviews and field notes.

From the frames of analysis, domains are created based on semantic relationships. Salient domains are used to identify common categories or themes. These phenomenological themes are used to develop a textural description of the essence of the lived experience of the participants (Hatch, 2002, p. 162). Phenomenological themes provide focus essential to capturing the fundamental meaning of the lived experience.

Research Questions

The following research questions guided this qualitative study:

1. How did students describe and understand the essence of their lived experiences with outdoor education?

2. What did students recall about their outdoor educational experiences and why did they recall those experiences?

3. How did the students see outdoor educational experiences being important to them in the future?

Context of the Study

Abi High School, a pseudonym used for the study site, was chosen for this study based on many similarities to the local school driving the need for this study. The significant difference between the two school districts was the utilization of school forest programming available to all students. Abi High School in Wisconsin was home to approximately 30 high school seniors. The demographic makeup of this school consisted mostly of White students and included a small number of Native American students. Subsidized lunch was used as an indicator of poverty status and almost half of the students at this school qualified for the subsidized lunch program (WINSS, 2008). The context of this phenomenology lies in the perceptions of 8 recently graduated high school seniors who attended Abi High School. The school district in which Abi High School is located owns an 80-acre school forest, which has been utilized for outdoor education experiences. These experiences have been a part of the school district's curriculum since 2000. The school forest is home to an outdoor classroom amid mixed hardwoods. Solin (2007) stated that school forests provide hands-on, experiential opportunities for students to learn about nature and about working together, and the main objective of school forest programming is for students to expand their understanding of themselves. School forests provide a location for outdoor educational experiences and the Abi School District supported those opportunities by providing all students with access to this resource.

Ethical Protection of Participants

Hatch (2002) stated that "we ask a lot when we ask individuals to participate in our qualitative studies" (p. 65). The protection of participant rights and the integrity of the research process were primary concerns in developing this research study. Creswell (2003) described measures to reduce the chances for ethical issues to develop. These measures included identifying the problem and the purpose of the study, gaining informed consent, respecting the participants by assessing and accommodating potential risks, using thoughtful written language, and refraining from unethical practices when reporting findings. In order to ensure the protection of participants, an approved human research protection training course with the National Institutes of Health was completed in order "to implement research procedures and designs that maximize the benefits and minimize the risks associated with research participation" (Walden University, 2009). Ethical issues were addressed by obtaining approval through Walden University's IRB process. The approval number for the IRB was 07-09-10-0355340. The function of the

IRB was to ensure that the research complied with the ethical standards of both Walden University and United States federal regulations. All procedures outlined in the IRB application were followed. I treated the individual participants with respect and sensitivity throughout data collection. Although the characteristics of participants may have placed them into a protected category without my knowledge, this study did not put their health at risk nor did it breach their safety or privacy. Full disclosure of the intent of the research and the voluntary nature of participation were made evident.

The district superintendent approved access to the site and the generation of a pool of participants. The pool of participants for this study consisted of recently graduated high school students who had reached the state's legal age of majority. A pool of potential participants was generated by a classroom teacher who also served as the school forest program coordinator. This pool of participants was approved by the district superintendent. All parents of potential participants were contacted via telephone to initiate consent to participate. Each of the parents contacted indicated that their child had reached the age of 18, so all contact with potential participants was made directly with them. During the initial conversation with the students, an explanation of the purpose of the research and an invitation to participate were discussed. If the student indicated that they would be willing to participate, an interview appointment was made and copies of the consent form along with an appointment reminder were mailed to them. Written permission from the district superintendent along with sample consent forms can be found in Appendix B.

Participant consent forms were discussed prior to the beginning of the interviews. Confidentiality of the participants was protected. When participant assent forms were signed, each participant was assigned a participant code. A record of all the participants' names along their codes was created at the beginning of the interview process and destroyed after completing all follow-up interviews. Initial semistructured interviews lasted approximately one hour. Following each interview, the digital recording was sent electronically to the transcriptionist, who had signed a confidentiality agreement (Appendix C). The only participant identifier on the recording was the participant code. Upon receipt of the transcript, I checked it for accuracy using the digital recording and the field notes. Participants had the opportunity to review the transcripts before they were used for analysis and helped verify the accuracy of the interpretation of the transcripts.

Role of the Researcher

Van Manen (1990) posited, "from a phenomenological point of view, to do research is always to question the way we experience the world, to want to know the world in which we live as human beings" (p. 5). I was a secondary school science teacher working in a small, rural high school. I had 20 years of experience working with students in the age group making up the participant pool for this study. I had worked in the capacity of school forest coordinator for six years. In this role, I provided environmental education activities in outdoor settings for K-8 students and directed the physical infrastructure of school forest resources in support of educational goals. I was not an employee of the study site so my professional roles did not affect data collection except for providing me with the necessary experience of working with and relating to this age group of students. My role in this research was as the writer and the investigator. I created the interview instrument and conducted.

My belief that the natural environment empowers people was fostered throughout my adolescence. Van Manen (1990) stated "to be aware of the structure of one's own experience of a phenomenon may provide the researcher with clues for orienting oneself to the phenomenon and thus to all other stages of phenomenological research" (p. 57). It is with this need for awareness of my orientation to the phenomenon that I spent time reflecting on my own experience and its influence on my life by asking myself if there was something essential to the experience of outdoor educational activities based on my personal understandings of the phenomenon. Moustakas (1994) stated that phenomenological research must "grow out of an intense interest in a particular problem or topic. Personal history brings the core of the problem into focus" (p. 104). My experience with the natural environment empowered me and inspired me to learn more about how to bring this same empowerment to my students.

Researcher bias was bracketed though the process of epoche, which is a suspension of all judgments about the topic of the study. Moustakas (1994) directed my efforts to revisit the phenomena through fresh eyes "from the vantage point of a pure or transcendental ego" (p. 33). I recognized my personal biases because of the role that the natural environment has played in providing a foundational strength in facing adversities in my life. This connection provided me with self-confidence and a sense of wonder about the world. This passion for the natural environment guided academic and personal choices. I embraced the process of epoche to ensure that personal biases did not influence the interview process or the interpretations of the participants' description of their lived experiences. A peer reviewer was also utilized to minimize the potential of bias.

Criteria for Selecting Participants

A purposeful sampling approach was used in the selection of participants. The primary criteria for participation in this study included graduation from the study site, a history of participating in outdoor educational experiences, and a willingness to participate in the study. The pool of participants at the study site consisted of 26 students who met the first criterion of senior status and the second criterion of participating in outdoor educational experiences. Each of these 26 students was invited to participate in the study and 8 volunteered to participate. In a phenomenology, the sample size was less important than the richness of the information obtained from the participants (Creswell, 1998, 2003; Hatch, 2002; Merriam, 2002; Patton, 2002). Creswell stated that there can be great variation in sample size in a phenomenological study. The depth of the information from each participant was more important than the number of participants since the intent was not to generalize the findings to the entire population.

Data Collection Procedures

To answer the research questions, data collection was completed through semistructured interviews. Below is an explanation of the data collection procedures and instruments.

Interview Process

The interview as a data collection device is an important source of information. Hatch (2002) stated

qualitative interviewers create a special kind of speech event during which they ask open-ended questions, encourage informants to explain their unique perspectives on the issues at hand, and listen intently for special language and other clues that reveal meaning structures informants use to understand their

worlds. (p. 23)

This interview process allows a researcher to develop a richer picture of the phenomenon under study because the story is being told in the voice of the participant. Gillham (2005) found "the element of professional impersonality (in the sense of not being in a personal relationship) seems to facilitate rather than inhibit disclosure" (p. 10). Participants may be more open to providing meaningful information when asked by the researcher than they might be when speaking generally in other situations.

Open-ended questions allow the participant to determine the answer. Gillham (2005) described the relationship between the researcher and the participant as a responsive, interactive exchange allowing for adjustment, clarification, and exploration while providing structure and purpose to the context of the interview. The semistructured interview process provided a rich picture of the phenomenon under study because the story was told in the voice of the participants. As suggested by Gillham (2005), questions for the interview protocol were constructed to facilitate data collection and were based on the research questions and the literature review. A brainstormed list of questions was edited for content, clarity, relevance, and redundancy. A draft of the interview protocol was presented to two colleagues for feedback, and changes were made to ensure it provided an opportunity for the participants to explore their lived experiences of the essence of the phenomenon. The interview protocol can be found in Appendix B.

During the summer of 2010, interviews were conducted in the school district's conference room. The conference room location provided minimal distractions and privacy for the interview. Interviews were scheduled with adequate time for reflection between each session. The interview began with an introduction. The ethical rights of the participants and expectations of the participants were reiterated. If the participant still agreed to participate in the study, the digital audio recorder was started and the interview commenced. Written field notes were kept during and following each interview. At the conclusion of each interview, the participants were thanked and asked if they would like to review a copy of the interview transcript. During the data analysis of each interview, follow-up interviews were scheduled and conducted, as needed, to ensure data saturation and as part of member checking. Phone and face-to-face interviews were scheduled into the summer until all data collection and member-checking were completed.

Data Analysis

The purpose of data analysis in hermeneutic phenomenological research was the determination and explication of the essential meaning of a lived experience. The process of developing an understanding of the lived experience of outdoor educational experiences was accomplished through an analytic analysis of the data. Van Manen (1990) stated "the insight into the essence of a phenomenon involves a process of reflectively appropriating, of clarifying, and of making explicit the structure of meaning of the lived experience" (p. 77). The process of developing an understanding of the lived experience of outdoor educational experiences was accomplished through an analysis of the data. Throughout the analysis process, a researcher's journal was kept that will document the thought processes used throughout the analysis of the data.

The process that was used to explore the themes in this study followed the framework described by Hatch (2002) who conceptualized data analysis as systematically asking questions of data in order to develop phenomenological themes. Through this data analysis, I was involved in exploring the themes that "embodied and dramatized in the evolving meanings and imagery of the work" (Van Manen, 1990, p. 78) in order to clarify the nature of the lived experience.

Starting analysis early in the data collection phase allowed the data to shape the direction of future data collection and improved the quality of the research (Hatch, 2002; Van Manen, 1990). Analysis of the data began as soon as possible following the collection of each data set. The analysis process was completed for the initial interview and repeated for each interview and each follow-up interview thereafter. Data collection continued until the research question had been answered.

At every interview, field notes were recorded and immediately following the interview, these field notes were transcribed into a word processor along with a reflection of the interview noting some initial thoughts. When the transcribed interview was completed, the interview and field notes were read in their entirety at the beginning of the analytic data analysis process as prescribed by Hatch (2002). The holistic review of each interview was done frequently throughout the data reduction process as each reading brought new insights based on the analysis of the data and the collection of new data. When individual transcripts were returned from the transcriptionist, they were sent to the participant for verification via e-mail as that was the method selected by each participant. If the participants wished to correct or clarify anything in the transcript, they had an opportunity to do so. The transcript, with any corrections and clarifications requested by the participant, and its accompanying field notes was entered into Atlas.ti software. Atlas.ti software was chosen for this study because of its ability to organize the large quantities of data generated through the data collection process and its ability to generate graphic organizers displaying semantic relationships. Creswell (2007) and Hatch (2002) listed advantages of computer software use, which included the ability to organize and store large amounts of data. This software encouraged the researcher to look closely at the data during coding processes and featured concept mapping features to enable the researcher to find relationships that might otherwise have been lost among the large quantities of data. Disadvantages included having to learn the software program. Computer software may also appear to put a barrier between the researcher and the data.

Using the Atlas.ti software, codes were applied to facilitate the development of a statement about the essence of the outdoor educational experience. Codes for frames of analysis were based on descriptive coding in which information was classified on a literal level. Domains were coded based on interpretive coding, which classifies information according to what it signifies. Semantic relationships were coded using pattern codes, which classify motifs found within the data.

After a close reading of the transcripts and field notes, frames of analysis were identified as prescribed by Hatch (2002) in his inductive analysis model. Frames of analysis are conceptual categories, the "segments, items, incidents, meaning units, or analysis units" (Tesch, 1990, p. 116). The frames of analysis provided the parameters on how the data were examined. The data and the frames of analysis changed throughout the analysis process. Based on the review of the literature and interview data, the importance of outdoor educational experiences as related to cognition, to psychological well-being, to creative expression, and with experiential learning guided the development of frames of reference/conceptual categories. The identification of semantic relationships between these categories led to the creation of domains.

The next steps using Hatch's (2002) inductive analysis process was to create domains based on semantic relationships discovered through the identification of the frames of analysis. "Domains can be categories that are understood by large numbers of people with common cultural understandings, or they can be categories that are developed within smaller groups with specialized interest and needs" (p. 165). Semantic relationships included strict inclusion, spatial, cause-effect, rationale, location for action, function, means-end, sequence, and attribution. The domains were expressed graphically by listing included terms and linking them using the semantic relationships. Domains which could not be linked were put aside in the next step of the analysis process, which was to select salient domains.

Using the graphic organizer, preliminary judgments were made concerning which domains were important to this study. The goal of this data reduction process was to narrow the focus of the data analysis process in order to get closer to the essence of the experience. The process was iterative and was refined as new data from additional interviews and follow-up interviews were collected. Hatch (2002) stated, "the process of searching and coding within salient domains will lead you to look more closely at your data and give you a better sense of the richness and importance of the domains you are finding" (p. 169). For each salient domain, the data were reviewed to find examples of the relationships.

The next step in Hatch's (2002) analytical analysis process was to ensure that the domains were supported by the data and to search for examples of data that did not support the domains. "This step involves examining the quality of the data that have been included in constructing your domains" (p. 170). When analysis indicated that elements in the domain were continuously repeated, that was evidence that a point of saturation has been reached and further data collection was not necessary. It was also important to make a systematic attempt to explore non-supportive data by asking specifically of each frame of analysis what did not fit with the established domains. The search for discrepant cases was important in the analytic process. When identified, a close examination of the non-supportive data were necessary to determine if the contradiction could be explained within the parameter of the domain or if the domain needed to revised or eliminated. Outliers or discrepant cases were included in the presentation of data and in final discussions.

The final step searched for phenomenological themes across domains. In this step, I looked for connections among the domains, taking a holistic look at the patterns and linkages amongst the data to find out what it all means (Hatch, 2002). Data excerpts were selected, which supported the identified phenomenological themes.

Trustworthiness of the Study

Validation of qualitative research is often referred to as the trustworthiness of a study. Lincoln and Guba (1985) used terms such as credibility, authenticity, and confirmability. A strategy for validation of qualitative studies is member-checking in which the researcher discusses interpretations of data and findings with the participants (Creswell, 2007). Participants were invited to participate in member-checking to verify the interview transcripts and preliminary interpretations. This was addressed during the study through three follow-up interviews conducted with participants. During these follow-up interviews, participants were asked to clarify parts of the transcript that were recorded as inaudible and to clarify some of their responses. A peer review was conducted at the end of the study to gauge whether the analysis and interpretations were free from bias and were "plausible based on the data" (Merriam, 2002, p. 26). The peer reviewer was utilized to read through the analysis of the data, the summary of the identified phenomenological themes, and the final statement about the essence of the outdoor educational experience. Discrepancies were identified and revised.

Reliability for this research was achieved using audit trails as recommended by Lincoln and Guba (1985). This included checking transcripts to ensure accurate transcription and protecting all of the raw data including the audiotapes and the field notes. In addition, a researcher's journal was kept to document the data reduction, analysis, and synthesis thought processes.

Summary of Methodology

This qualitative hermeneutic phenomenology research was conducted during the summer of 2010. The constructivist paradigm guided the development of the methodology. In a search for the answers to the central research question, participants were interviewed using an interview protocol that included probing questions to provide insights into their lived experience of the phenomenon. Three follow-up interviews were conducted with participants were conducted in order to ensure saturation of data. IRB approval was obtained, confidentiality was assured, and all data were kept secured to ensure participant protection. Trustworthiness was addressed through the process of member-checking and peer review. Reliability was enhanced by audio taping interviews and by checking transcripts against the audiotape to ensure accurate transcription. Additionally, I used field notes to check against the transcripts to ensure an accurate representation of the interview was used in the data analysis and maintained a researcher's journal documenting thought processes throughout the analysis process. Section 3 provided the details of the methodology to be used in this study. Section 4 of this study reports the results and findings of the qualitative data in this study.

Section 4: Results

A qualitative phenomenological study was chosen to describe the lived experiences of eight students' outdoor educational experiences. The purpose of this phenomenological study was to explore the essence of meaning in the lived experiences of recent high school graduates who had taken part in outdoor educational experiences. This information may help school districts make informed decisions on the allocation of money for educational programs. The hermeneutic phenomenological tradition was the most appropriate for this study because this methodology seeks a composite meaning of several individuals' description of their lived experiences as interpreted by me.

Data Collection

The participants were students who graduated high school during the spring of 2010. The participants had experienced educational programming in an outdoor setting. The person designated by the superintendent of schools at the study site provided contact information for the pool of participants meeting selection criteria. From the pool of 26 participants, I was able to make initial phone contact with 15 of the parents. I explained the research project to the parents. I stressed the confidential and voluntary nature of participation during this initial phone conversation. Each parent was reminded that since the school year had recently ended, the newly graduated student would need transportation to the school for the interview. All the parents provided me with oral permission to contact the student and informed me that transportation to the interview site would not be a problem. As it turned out, each of the students in the participant pool had reached the age of consent at the time of initial contact so signed parental consent was not necessary.

I then contacted each potential participant by phone and explained the purpose of the study, the expectations of the participant, the confidential and voluntary nature of the study and the risks and benefits of participating in the study. Each participant was informed that the interview would be held at the school and that he or she would need to provide his or her own transportation. After this phone contact, eight students agreed to participate in the study and an interview was scheduled with each. A student consent form along with a reminder of the interview time and place was mailed to the participant. The student participant was reminded to bring the consent form with him or her to the interview. No data were collected during this call.

A school district conference room was made available for the interview process. The district serving as a site for this study consisted of a single building serving the elementary and secondary student population. In addition, this building served as a community center housing the town library and hosting many community functions. The availability of this conference room provided a convenient meeting place that provided a familiar, safe environment, which would encourage an honest sharing of lived experiences. The interviews were scheduled to last for one hour. A minimum of one hour was scheduled between interviews to ensure an adequate amount of time was available to be used as a buffer between participant interviews. This time allotment ensured that participants did not meet with each other prior to the interview process and that the participant's interview began at the appointed time. The time between interviews also provided me time to review and maintain my field notes. Participants were able to choose interview times that were convenient to their schedules. The interview schedule was kept on a password protected personal digital assistant (PDA).

Prior to beginning the interviews, I spent time reflecting on the research questions and interview protocol in an attempt to bracket my own ideas during the interview and during data analysis. As discussed in section 3, epoche is the suspension of judgment. Husserl (1970) believed that through the process of bracketing pre-existing beliefs, the researcher would be able to suspend judgment and the essence of the phenomenon would become clearly evident. Moustakas (1994) stated that the "value of the epoche principle is that it inspires one to examine biases and enhances one's openness even if a perfect and pure state is not achieved" (p. 61). Giorgi (2006) questioned Moustakas's use of the epoche process and recommended "noting the presence of the biases as they function" (p. 310). Van Manen (1990) used the term bracketing to describe the process of epoche. Bracketing "describes the act of suspending one's various beliefs in the reality of the natural world in order to study the essential structures of the world" (p. 175).

Phenomenological methodology lacks a clearly definitive explication. There is not a single, correct interpretation of the data. This varied approach to interpretation creates an environment in which phenomenological researchers need to make practical applications on the basis the ideas of the scholars in the field (Van Manen, 1990). Therefore, I chose to spend time in reflection concerning my own biases and opinions about this study. The importance of the process me was accentuated when I began the epoche process; the location I had unintentionally chosen for reflection was the outdoors, surrounded by the sensory stimuli of nature. These biases were not shared initially with the participants but, in some instances, were shared following the participants' responses, often with an opposing point of view in order to provide the participant choices and further explore their lived experience.

At the beginning of each interview, I reviewed the interview protocol, the research questions, and the purpose of the study in order to keep these in the forefront of the interview process. When each participant arrived for their interview, I greeted him or her at the door of the conference room, introduced myself, confirmed their identity, and thanked them for their participation. I explained to each participant that I would be using a digital voice recorder in order to record everything he or she said and asked if he or she was comfortable with having the interview recorded. Each participant stated that having the interview digitally recorded would not bother him or her. I took time to explain the purpose of the study and to review the consent form to ensure that the participant was aware of the confidential nature, the right to withdraw at any time from the study, and the requirements of the participants--in particular the review of the transcript and the probable need for follow-up questions. I noted their request for follow-up contact and all participants wanted the transcript emailed in an electronic format. Adam, Betty, and David requested future contact to be conducted through email correspondence (all participant names are pseudonyms). The other participants requested future contact to be conducted through telephone. I informed the participants that what they had to share was important and reassured them that there were no wrong answers. In addition, I reiterated that if the participant was uncomfortable or simply did not wish to answer a question, that he or she simply had to inform me of their choice and I would honor all requests. I completed this introductory phase of the interview process by explaining that the interview would be conversational in nature, which reflected Rubin and Rubin's (2005) interview process called responsive interviewing. I then activated the digital voice recorder and the interview began.

The interview proceeded following the interview protocol. Probing questions were added to each question to ensure that the participants' lived experiences were fully explored. Field notes were recorded throughout the interview and were used to help inform which probe would be the most useful in helping the participant share his or her story. The field notes were also used to record my personal thoughts throughout the interview so that I could remain impartial during the process but still reflect on those ideas following the interview. At the conclusion of the interview, I thanked the participants and reminded them that I would be sending the transcription of the interview to them within one week. They were instructed to note any issues they had with the transcript and to include anything they wanted added or deleted. If there were any changes, they were instructed to send the requested changes back to me by replying to the email. After the participant left, I checked the interview schedule to make sure that I was aware of the time the next participant would arrive. The time between interviews ranged from one to three hours. During this time, field notes were transcribed into a word processing document and the digital audio recordings were transferred to a password protected jump drive. The jump drive was personally delivered to the transcriptionist at the end of each interview day.

Within one week the transcriptionist called me to personally pick up the word processed transcripts on the original jump drives. After I compared the transcription with the original audio recording to ensure accuracy, I e-mailed the transcription to the interviewee for review and reiterated the instructions for review and return if there were changes. I also reminded them that I would be calling with follow-up questions within the next few weeks.

I used the time between completing the initial interview process and receiving the transcribed interviews to review the field notes. During this review, several main ideas expressed throughout all of the interviews became apparent. When the interview transcripts were available, I entered them into the Atlas.ti software program along with the field notes I had previously transcribed. After working with the data for several days, I called each participant to verify that they were comfortable with their responses and asked several follow-up questions to ensure that my understandings of how their responses and my preliminary conclusions about the composite meanings of the data were on target.

Tracking the Data

The interview process and protocol were approved for use following an oral presentation by my doctoral committee and Walden University's Institutional Review Board. The Atlas.ti software program provided structure to the analysis of the qualitative data in a creative yet systematic way. The tools embedded within the software package allowed me to use an intuitive, holistic approach to visualize the complex relationships uncovered throughout the analysis. Prior to the receipt of the transcripts, each question in the approved protocol along with the field notes were carefully reviewed in order to create the preliminary codes that were used in identifying the responses to each question. As soon as they were available, the transcripts of the interviews were entered into the Atlas.ti software program as primary documents. The preliminary descriptive codes facilitated the initial sorting of the data and provided a firm foundation for getting started. The preliminary codes were not exhaustive; several more codes were added throughout the processing of the first four interviews. No additional codes were needed in the coding of the final interview providing an indication that data saturation had been reached. The complete list of the codes used is found in Appendix C.

When I received the received the completed transcripts of the interviews, I uploaded them as primary documents into the Atlas.ti software. I read closely for key ideas and phrases in the written text and coded them using the previously identified codes. After assigning codes to the primary documents, I used the software to examine the *groundedness* of the codes, which refers to determining the number of quotations assigned to a given code (Muhr, 2004). The codes for cognition and experiential learning were the most frequently used codes. Using the network editor included in the software, I linked the codes into networks in order to identify the domains, which classified information according to what it signified. Domains were identified based on the research questions and the interview protocol. The domains include the experience in context, the detail of the school forest experience, and a reflection of the school forest experience. The network of nodes was identified through an analysis of the data and is further described in the findings which follow.

Participant Profiles

All of the participants in this study were given pseudonyms to ensure confidentiality. Table 1 displays the attributes of these recent high school graduates.

Table 1

Participant Attributes

ID	Age	Sex	Race
Adam	18	M	Native American
Betty	18	F	White
Carrie	18	F	White
David	18	M	White
Evan	19	M	White
Greta	18	F	White
Harry	19	M	Native American

Participant Adam was a confident 18-year-old Native American man, who had graduated from high school in June, 2010. Adam came to the interview dressed in a jeans and a sweatshirt with the words "Native Pride" across the front. He was well-spoken and extremely polite with a ready smile and openness to sharing his experiences. He expressed pride in his culture even while relating some of the difficulties currently being experienced by many of the young people in his tribe. Adam lived with his father and stepmother. Adam maintained close family ties with his mother and extended family including grandparents, aunts, and uncles. Adam described his childhood as "growing up and being outside with my family, playing in the woods and going camping and fishing a lot". Adam also participated in tribal activities including traditional dancing and pow wows and planned on working with the tribe's natural resources department.

Participant Betty was a White, 18-year-old female who graduated high school a few weeks before the interview process began. Betty was a small, slender young woman who exhibited a quiet demeanor throughout the interview process. She wore jeans and a plain pink t-shirt to the initial interview. Betty was open about sharing the difficulties of being raised in a dysfunctional family in which both parents were alcoholics. She had one sister who was cognitively disabled. In sharing her story, Betty stated, "I have a lot of good memories about outdoors. I love being outside. That is one of my favorite places to be." Betty shared many stories about how nature provided a stable, safe environment she used to bridge the communication gap with her alcoholic father because of their shared love of the outdoors.

Participant Carrie was an 18-year-old White female. Carrie had recently graduated high school where she served for four years on the school's student council, her final year as student council president. Carrie served as captain of her varsity volleyball team. Carrie wore jeans and a volleyball team shirt to the interview. While she felt that the school forest experiences she had participated in were valuable, she was not convinced that she had anything of value to share. After some casual discussion to put her at ease, Carrie stated, "Being outdoors provided some place to run, to throw a ball without getting yelled at." Carrie had an identical twin sister, lived with both her parents, and moved to the school she had just graduated from when she was 12.

Participant David was an 18-year-old White man who enjoyed outdoor sports such as golf, baseball, fishing and hunting. David graduated from high school one month before the initial interview. David entered the interview room wearing a ball cap and dressed in jeans and a t-shirt that endorsed a local sports team. David was confident and well-spoken. He explained that his best memories of growing up were time spent hunting and fishing with his dad and grandfather. David referred several times to the quiet, relaxing atmosphere of being outdoors. Most of David's elective coursework was in technology education. David was employed with his father's logging company and planned on making a career in logging.

Participant Evan was a 19-year-old White man. He also enjoyed hunting and fishing with his family. Evan was a tall, solidly built young man who played high school football play. Evan was one of five children and lived with his parents. His future plans included obtaining a college degree in a science-related field. Evan characterized himself as a loner who liked to explore his natural environment. He shared, "I like being outside where I can see and smell and touch and explore my surroundings."

Participant Greta was an 18-year-old White female. Greta arrived dressed in jeans and a hooded sweatshirt bearing a sports logo. She graduated from high school the previous month and worked in a local supermarket, earning money for college in the fall. Greta had a positive attitude about the interview process and easily shared her experiences with outdoor education. She participated in leadership activities at the school forest and talked about how she would miss living in a wood, rural environment when she left for college. One of her favorite hobbies was nature photography.

Participant Harry was a 19-year-old Native American man. Harry wore his long hair in a braid down his back. He shared his desire to obtain an education so that he could come back and become the tribal chairperson. Harry had played basketball all four years of high school. Following his junior, Harry received a large sum of money from the tribe on his eighteenth birthday and spent time traveling around the world. He returned to school in the fall with a renewed sense of responsibility. Harry was an active member of his tribe and enjoyed spending time at powwows and dancing. Harry's family was very dysfunctional and both parents were alcoholics but Harry was dedicated to mentoring other troubled youth with similar challenges obtain the skills necessary to be successful in school. Like most of the interviewees, Harry found emotional strength in his relationship with nature.

Findings

The summary of the findings as presented here were grouped based on the research questions that guided this study. Quotes were kept as close as possible to the original transcript in order to retain the flavor of the conversational style of the participant. I chose this format because it kept the focus on the composite meaning of the participants' description of their experiences. The convergence of the responses in these sections led me to uncover four themes: *family experiences and free play, personal growth and leadership, values, and cognitive freedom.* Each of these themes helped describe the essence of the phenomenon.

Research Question One

The first research question asked "How did students describe and understand the essence of their lived experiences with outdoor education?" This question sought to build an understanding of the essence of the participants' lived experience with outdoor education through an exploration of their earliest memories of learning something outdoors and what they recalled about their first experience at the school forest. The first theme was rooted in family experiences and a sense of freedom in outdoor play (Adam, Betty, David, Evan, & Fred). Six of the participants' earliest memories of learning outdoors were based in their experiences of growing up in a rural area characterized by mixed hardwood forests. "Just growing up and being outside. Playing in the woods and stuff like that. Going camping a lot and being outside with my family" (Adam). Five participants shared similar stories about growing up in a natural environment. "I just liked playing around, playing tag. The fresh air makes you feel good" (Carrie). "My best memory was probably opening morning of deer season with my grandpa, sitting on the stand" (David). Spending time with family members was an important part of the early experiences expressed by the participants. When asked about what he had learned during his early outdoor experiences, one participant replied that he had "learned a lot logging with [his] grandparents and uncle. A lot of different species of wood and all different kinds of stuff they're used for" (David).

Betty discussed her conviction that her outdoor educational experiences were responsible for helping her maintain a functional relationship with her alcoholic parents who were in recovery status at the time of this study. She indicated that free play in outdoor settings was an integral part of her life. According to Payne (1996), families living in poverty status have a lack of emotional, mental, spiritual, physical, and role models resources, which would allow them to escape the cycle of poverty. Betty described how it was her relationship with her environment that provided the resources necessary for her to attain the skills and resources necessary for her to set high standards for herself and for her future. Outdoor educational experiences allowed her to tap into those skills and resources so that she was able to attain success in her public school. Responses from the other participants echoed the importance of outdoor educational experiences in providing leadership skills that would promote success beyond high school supported by the concepts of academic resilience.

Participants often used sensory terms to describe their early experiences. One participant went so far as saying "Earliest memories are all bad ones. Those are all the memories you have. Probably age 4 playing baseball with my brother. He hit me in the head with a baseball bat" (David). From the field notes, the participant was smiling and laughing about the initial part of this quote. When further questioned about the incident, the participant described having a great relationship with all of five of his siblings. "My brothers and sister and I spent lots of time hanging around outside 'cause my mom would always tell us to go outside and play" (David). Participants described the quiet of nature as stimulation to sensory experiences. "Like smell, what you hear about what goes on. Sometimes during the day you can't hear about what goes on in the woods, but when you go out in the dark there's a bunch of sounds like from wild animals waking up and stuff like that" (Adam). Sensory experiences were also brought up by another participant who stated that

> You need to be quiet to observe everything around you in the wild. Just walking you see a lot, but sitting there listening, seeing, feeling the wind, you can definitely learn a lot more than just walking through the wild. There's so many more things to pick up on. Getting to hear the rustle of leaves way back then when you walk over there you can find what it is. It's different. (David)

When a participant shared a story of going fishing with his grandfather, he said that "You get to try to catch a big one and you get to be outside in the sun and relax. It's usually peaceful out there. If you go to smaller lakes there's nobody out there to make a bunch of noise. It's nice to get away" (Fred). Long-term memory is closely related to the sensory nature of the experience. These responses are consistent with brain-based learning as discussed in the literature review (Gulpinar, 2005).

Adam and Harry are Native American students. When Harry discussed his relationship with nature, he expressed:

> In homes of Native Americans, they live off of fish and deer. It kind of takes away of our traditions of what we do hunting, fishing, and gathering. It takes away from what our culture kind of, we've kind of moved away from it. I don't see as many people hunting as they used to. Just lately logging took over my area. It's changed a lot too.

Adam also discussed his relationship to nature as part of his relationship with his family. "My grandpa and his brother are big with telling generational stories. They're trying to teach the young ones, some of the young ones they're having problems. They don't listen to them anymore." Adam also stated that his outdoor educational experiences had "helped me understand more of our generational stories. I appreciate my culture a lot more than I used to. I didn't appreciate it as much, but looking at it right now, it's kind of falling apart." Adam credited his family relationships with his strength of character and his personal and educational successes.

The literature discussed racial disproportionality as prevalent among Native American students. This disproportionality is due, in part, to the disparity of early learning opportunities available to minority youth. It is also due do to the cultural learning differences that conflict with the Eurocentric education system prevalent in American public education. The responses as revealed indicated that early experiences of free play within the context of outdoor environments where indicative of a positive self-esteem and academic success.

While demographic information about the participants was not sought, the participants did share several relevant insights into their potential risk status. As an unintentional consequence of the interview process, Adam and Harry disclosed their Native American heritage and Betty disclosed the socioeconomic status of her family. Adam and Harry both commented on the successful use of outdoor education as a reinforcement of their cultural teachings. The outdoor educational experiences provided relevance to the classroom experiences and it was the outdoor educational experiences that provided connections between the Eurocentric classroom teachings and the generational stories told to them by the tribal elders. Fixico (2003) described this connection as balance, balance between self, family, community, other communities, the spiritual world, and the universe.

Research Question Two

The second research question asked "What did students recall about their outdoor educational experiences and why did they recall those experiences?" Additionally, this research question sought recollections of how participants applied something they learned at the school forest to their school work. All participants had been involved in one or more outdoor learning opportunities at their school district's school forest, which serves the district as an outdoor classroom. These experiences were rooted in a holistic learning environment where cognition was based on experiential learning. The theme of leadership was revealed throughout the interview process. One participant recalled that the best part of his school forest experience was "helping kids with what we're learning about. What they had to look for. Without my knowledge of knowing what stuff was and what they had to look for" (Adam). Basically, Adam discovered that one of the best ways of learning something was to teach it. He went on to share that "I like hands-on. Getting out and doing what you learn about. Hands-on is my thing for everything." The experiential learning pedagogy was a consistent benefit of outdoor educational experiences in all of the interviews. Participant comments frequently referenced hands-on learning opportunities. Betty commented:

> It's definitely more open and people are different. Some people are more visual, some are more hands-on, some are more just listening and they got it. But, for people that are more hands-on and need to see what they're doing and be more interactive, like one-on-one or with the whole group, it's a good experience for people to go out there.

Four of the participants' memories of their experiences were seldom of definitive learning experiences but what they recall is that they learned. "Last year we learned to do some core samples out there and figure out how many trees were in a square mile. I've learned a lot out there. Just random stuff" (Carrie). Three other participants recalled more specific activities such as "we went out there when we built the bunk beds out of logs. We went out there and built all of that, grilled out, and had a good time" (David). The positive attitudes towards learning during these outdoor educational experiences helped describe why the students recalled those experiences.

Students recalled outdoor experiences that encouraged questions about their lived experiences. For example, Greta recalled her swimming experiences. She remembered "swimming" and "opening [her] eyes once." She added, "There were four Northern [fish] just looking at me. It freaked me out the first time. I thought that was interesting. Why are they just staring at me?" Adam recalled experiences that were unique and encouraged thinking on a deeper level. He stated:

> Learning and seeing things that you don't see every day. You do your thing, but when you see something cool from nature you take your time and look at it and you just soak it in and just love it. Makes you stop in your tracks and you're like "Oh that's cool" and just sit there. Like you're always on a time schedule every day and when you think about nature you just stop and want to sit there all day and look at it.

As indicated by the learning theories (Dewey, 1938; Freire, 2008; Gardner, 2005; & Vygotsky, 1956), students reported that thinking critically, questioning observations, and exploring possibilities increased their learning. Dewey (1938) believed that learning best happened in a realm in which communication was the basis of effective education and that teachers should provide experiences upon which students can build understanding. Freire discussed how students exposed to a situation built their understanding of the situation through discussion and reflection. In addition, Vygotsky believed that it was imperative that teachers recognize the culture that provides the basis of the child's learning style and contributes to the child's intellectual development.

Moran, Kornhaber, and Gardner (2006) promoted the idea that humans exhibit several intelligences including linguistic, logical—mathematical, musical, spatial, bodily—kinesthetic, interpersonal, intrapersonal, and naturalistic. Louv (2005) identified nature-deficit disorder as a condition resulted from a human alienation from nature and provided several examples of how the lack of exposure or an enriched exposure to nature can influence the ability of people to learn. Brain-based learning theories advocate for the creation of an emotional and social climate for learning, the creation of rich, complex and realistic experiences with opportunities to reflect, find, and construct meaningful connections and the creation of ways to consolidate learning by constructing mental models. The perceptions of the participants supported these ideas promoted through the literature. Students discussed the sensory nature of their learning experiences and how activities at the school forest provided those sensory opportunities. Personal growth and leadership skills were identified as byproducts of these experiences.

Personal growth and leadership were common themes throughout the interviews with Adam, Betty, David, Fred, and Greta. "My experiences at the school forest helped me gain confidence in myself" (Greta). "My experiences with nature have made me look deeper into someone. Not just outside features" (Fred). The outdoor educational experiences were consistently more about growing as a person than learning specific concepts. After reflecting on his school forest experiences, Adam stated, "I'm kind of a better person lately. Kind of a more happier guy lately." As I probed this comment further, in relation to Adam's Native American culture and if he felt that school forest experiences would help nullify some of the negative influences plaguing other young Native American youth, he stated that many young people on the reservation "have troubles. And they kind of don't care. It's got to change and it's got to become more of a caring more about where their living right" (Adam). He speculated that if outdoor educational experiences were made more available, maybe if we encouraged more traditional Native American activities in the school forest or if more outdoor educational activities were offered on the reservation that might help keep some of the Native

American youth focused on positive living. Adam stated that he would be working with the tribal center in the natural resources department following graduation.

David recalled his outdoor educational experiences. "They give you more responsibility out there. More trust. There's usually just one teacher out there so you get into groups and you go out and do what you've got to do" (David). Carrie also expressed the impact of her outdoor educational experiences: "Coming into high school, I was more of a shy person. Raise my hand just to talk. Didn't want to get talking during class, that kind of thing. Now, I think of myself more as a leader." When completing learning tasks at the school forest, one participant stated that being part of a team made her "feel like I was the kind of person that initiated, just took control and said this is what we need to do and go do whatever" (Betty). Leadership is an important trait along with confidence, trust, and responsibility that seem to be nurtured during outdoor educational experiences.

Betty discussed her learning style. Betty used her knowledge of her learning styles to find success in the traditional classroom.

I'm a very outdoorsy person. My last whole summer was spent scraping moss off of rocks for, that's what I did as a job. I sold moss and ginseng, hunting for wild ginseng, which I'm actually still making money off of, me and my boyfriend are. Leeches, I trap leeches. I put chicken livers in a sock, threw them in a bucket, and put that in the pond. I'd rather do anything outside than inside. It's nice to just get out there. And I do like the non-traditional learning versus your standard every day procedure.

Seven students described their preferred learning environment as "being outside, it makes it easier to learn, outside is better than being bricked in" (Harry). The theme of cognitive freedom was typified by Harry when he expanded his explanation of being bricked in to include both metaphorically, as it pertained to his creativity, and physically, as it pertained to the four walls of his classroom.

Experiential learning was mentioned by all eight of the participants as an important part of their cognitive skills. Outdoor education provided the structure for experiential learning to take place. "Just the laid back atmosphere of being outside and not in a cramped little classroom with however many students. We can have our little, you know, you can sit on the ground and get our butts dirty and it's okay" (Betty). Greta shared a story about learning about vernal pools and the life cycle of frogs. She stated that she "liked it because it was hands-on. It showed me that I'm more of a hands-on learner because I really got it." Another participant was an avid hunter and explained how he used a trigonometry lesson at the school forest to calculate angles for his hobby.

> I never thought I would actually use it until I was trying to figure out how well if you shot a one inch group at a hundred yards what that would be equivalent to at 900 yards using the angle. If it's a 1-to-1, 900 hundred yards is going to be nine inches. I really didn't think I was going to use it until then. (Harry)

The ability to transfer knowledge to new situations is an important yet common outcome when using experiential education. David explained his take on experiential education. "Right now I'm in biology and we're studying plants like how some flowers attract bees by scent. You can't really describe a scent unless you were able to smell the flower. That sweet smell." He built upon this idea when he shared "if you pretended to be a bee, you'd probably remember it a little better. It would be fun. It would be humorous."

Fred stated, "I think it really helps the kids to get out of the school and fresh air to

actually touch what they're talking about. You can sit there and study a biology book as

much as you want. You're not going to really know it until you see it." Participating in

real-world experiences took abstract ideas and turned them into concrete ideas was

considered a universal benefit of outdoor educational experiences among all the

participants.

Cognition is the way humans process thought and apply knowledge (Beard &

Wilson, 2006; Broda, 2007; Dewey, 1916; Knapp, 1996; Sobel, 2005). Improving

cognitive skills are key elements in the use of outdoor educational experiences. The main

purpose of outdoor education is the provision of meaningful experiences in natural

environments in order to complement classroom instruction. The responses indicated that

outdoor educational experiences, as related by the participants, dovetail with the

pedagogical construct of place-based education. Place-based education, as discussed in

the literature, puts contextual learning into the local culture and natural environment.

The constructs of place-based education are based on holistic, integrated, and meaningful

experiences that incorporate culture studies, nature studies, and real-world problem-

solving. Experiential learning is also closely aligned with outdoor educational

experiences and involves the active engagement of the learner. The characteristics of

relevance, relationships, and authentic, real-world experiences are indicative of

experiential education. Participant responses supported the ideals of place-based

educational strategies and experiential learning.

Outdoor education places an emphasis on both interpersonal and intrapersonal skills (Hill, 2007; Priest & Gass, 1997; Zink & Burrows, 2006). Increased leadership skills developed through outdoor educational experiences were common topics throughout the participant interviews. The role of the spiritual aspects of outdoor education, such as peacefulness, relaxation, the quietness of the spirit and the quietness of the environment, were found throughout the participant responses.

Participants revealed important insights into their cognitive processes. Cognition was related to early family memories, school forest experiences, and the planned use of school forest experiences into their futures. "I like hands-on. Getting out and doing what you learn about. Hands-on is my thing for everything" (Adam). In addition, Adam stated that "You see new things. Some things you can't experience inside like you do outside." He also provided further clarification of this idea when he stated that "like with fish, being able to look at the fish, real fish and learn about them outside." Six of the participants explained how being outside affected their cognitive processes. "Well even that [math] would be better to learn outside, I would think. We did do a fair amount of writing and stuff. To do it outside, it's just a whole different atmosphere. It's just nicer to learn out there" (Betty). Betty went on to explain the importance of interdisciplinary activities at the forest.

> [They] broaden your scope because when you're at school you think "I can do this, this, or this", but when you get out to the school forest and realize there's all these other things that you can do just forest related. There are still all sorts of other things that it [nature] opens your eyes to.

Being in an outdoor environment provided Betty with an opportunity to consider many alternative answers and to synthesize what she had learned into a new, higher level understanding of the concepts.

Carrie shared this explanation of how the school forest impacted her cognition. "When we're out there we're focused on getting our work done. It's pretty nice out there, even just to go on a walk while we were talking about ideas. Just to clear your mind, it helped." She went on to explain that she is

> not valedictorian, but I'm top 25% of my class. I'd say I'm more of a hands-on person, definitely. Because I can't just see someone do it and think that I know how to do it. I need to be able to do it myself, to know that I can do it later. Like math class. I can see him, I can follow the problems on the board, but later on if I don't do my own examples during class then it's gone from memory. I don't know because I didn't do it so I don't know how to do it. (Carrie)

School forest experiences provided this participant with a deeper understanding of her cognitive processes. She learned that she needed a hands-on learning environment, which provided opportunities to explore creative, innovative solutions in order to continue achieving a high level of success. David, Greta, and Harry shared similar stories about their cognitive processes.

Research Question Three

The third research question asked "How did the students see outdoor educational experiences being important to them in the future?" Values, another theme identified in this study, were described throughout this segment of the interview. Seven of the participants expressed an increased environmental awareness. "I think of nature, I need to take care of it more and not abuse it. It's here for us to survive" (Adam). This Native American participant elaborated with "Like for my kids how it's going to be with how pollution is right now, it's bad. And how with the logging industry it's where you're changing the environment all the time." One of the participants is pursuing an environmental related career. "I'm going for natural resources at [a technical college]. I'm going into the transfer program. I don't know what field I'm going into yet because there's so many interesting things to go into. Right now I'm eyeing the land surveying thing" (Adam). Adam expressed a desire to learn more about nature in an effort to return to his tribe so that he could mentor troubled Native American youth.

Although seven of the participants were not planning a career in an environmental field, all eight participants considered their experiences with outdoor education as influential on their value system. "I think personally I'm still going to hunt or fish or be in the outdoors, but more of my career is going to be in the city" (David). Five participants expressed the importance of bringing outdoor educational experiences to their successors. "Being a part of future generations makes it cool to help, to make it a better place" (Greta). Greta also shared that without the experiences in outdoor classrooms, "especially around here because it's all outdoors, you'd kind of be lost." She stated that students would not be able to fully appreciate the rural, forested ecosystem they lived in. Another student noticed that people from urban areas "who come up here just don't really care about it. They don't take care of anything, destroy it. Try to give them a better understanding to not destroy things, but just take care of it and it'll be around" (David). One participant grew up in a suburban area and, although he grew up with a big yard, he characterized his environment as "man-made" (Greta). In the future, this participant was planning to go into film making and saw his experiences in the school forest as creative inspiration for his art. "I want to create a film that contrasts the ideas of nature versus urban grit" (Greta). Students valued the relaxed, interdisciplinary nature of the outdoor experience and recognized their need to bring these experiences into their futures, no matter where that future takes them.

Discrepant Cases and Non-conforming Data

Hatch (2002) recommended that the researcher diligently and systematically search for data that challenged emerging frames of analysis. The search for these non-conforming or discrepant patterns required a purposeful inquiry of data that contradicted the findings (p. 158). One discrepant case emerged in this study involving participant Evan. Evan's attitude differed from the other participant's interviewed as he was the only participant to be ambivalent about participation in outdoor educational experiences, including those provided by the school. Evan stated that he felt more comfortable in traditional learning situations in the classroom. "You don't have all the resources available, like the internet." He talked about how the school forest experience provided an opportunity to "get around and do different stuff." Even though he expressed interest in hunting as a hobby, he stated, "Hunting is very aggravating, I don't have the patience for it." When responding to probes, Evan said he was a solitary, visual learner who would find increased value in outdoor educational experiences if there was more technology available.

The remaining seven participants expressed the value of outdoor educational experiences and wished they could participate in the outdoors more than in traditional classroom and work settings. For example, Adam expounded upon the value of outdoor educational experiences and how they have inspired him to pursue a career in natural resources. "I've been taking what I learn at school and I'm using it to take care of the baseball fields, and cleaning up trash from local parks, and now I'm eyeing land use planning for a career." Betty was disappointed because she has "had opportunities to go out there [school forest], but I don't like missing school to go out there because I'm not set to graduate and I'm having difficulties with math so I need to stay on that instead of going out. It would be more fun to go that route". Adam and Betty expressed the value they found in their outdoor educational experiences. These responses typified those of the seven students.

Evidence of Quality

Validity of this study was established using two methods. One of the strategies used for validation of this study was member-checking in which the researcher discusses interpretations of data and findings with the participants (Creswell, 2007). After the recordings were transcribed, they were sent to each participant in an email as requested by the participant. I gave them one week to review the transcript and then telephoned them to ask if they had any corrections or questions. I also took this opportunity to share some preliminary interpretations with the participants and to ask some follow-up questions. The participants acknowledged that they had received and read through the transcript. None had any corrections or questions. The follow-up questions clarified some unintelligible segments in the transcript and validated preliminary interpretations.

A second check on validity was accomplished through the use of a peer reviewer. The peer reviewer was provided with a copy of the transcripts, a copy of the findings and my preliminary statement about the essence of the outdoor educational experience. A video conference using Skype software was used to discuss and to clarify the questions generated by the review. While there were no fundamental changes that were made, the conference was invaluable in clarifying my preliminary interpretations. The next section will discuss how the findings were interpreted and the final statement about the essence of the outdoor educational experience along with recommendations for future research.

Section 5: Summary, Conclusion, and Recommendations

Overview of the Study

Outdoor educational experiences utilize the natural environment as an interactive, experiential learning classroom. The purpose of this study was to explore the lived experiences of participants who experienced outdoor educational experiences. To accomplish this, I conducted a phenomenological study to provide an opportunity to hear an account of the experience in the voices of the participants. The research questions that guided this study asked the following:

1. How did students describe and understand the essence of their lived experiences with outdoor education?

2. What did students recall about their outdoor educational experiences and why did they recall those experiences?

3. How did the students see outdoor educational experiences being important to them in the future?

A phenomenological study generates a composite meaning of several individuals' description of their lived experiences (van Manen, 1990, p. 10). I interviewed eight young adults who had recently graduated from a high school that utilized a school forest as an outdoor education classroom and incorporated outdoor educational experiences into their district's K-12 curriculum.

Using Hatch's (2002) inductive analysis process began with my repeated reading of the transcribed interviews and field notes, frames of analysis in the form of codes were developed. These codes were changed throughout the analysis process. After coding the interview transcripts, semantic relationships between the codes led to the creation of domains or categories, which were expressed graphically using the Atlas.ti software.

Using the graphic organizer, the goal of the data reduction process was to narrow the focus of the data analysis process in order to get closer to the essence of the experience. This process was iterative and was continued and refined as new data from additional interviews and follow-up interviews are collected. For each salient domain, the data were reviewed to find examples of the relationships.

A systematic attempt to explore discrepant cases by asking specifically of each frame of analysis what did not fit with the established domains. When identified, a close examination of the non-supportive data was necessary to determine if the contradiction could be explained within the parameter of the domain or if the domain needed to revised or eliminated. The final step searched for phenomenological themes across domains.

The findings of the study revealed insights into how students remembered their outdoor educational experiences. The findings include the following:

1. Family played an important role in providing early learning experiences in the natural environment.

2. The quality of the outdoor educational instruction was an important component in the positive perception of these experiences.

3. Outdoor educational instruction had a positive impact on the cognitive skills of the participants.

These findings were used to identify the themes of this study which included family experiences, personal growth and leadership, values, and cognitive freedom which describe the essence of the outdoor educational experience.

Interpretations of Findings

The interpretation of findings section of this study was organized according to the research questions. The patterns found in the findings associated with each research question were used to develop basic themes which were used to describe the essence of the participants' perception of their outdoor educational experiences.

Conclusion One – The Importance of Family and Free Play

The first research question asked how students described and understood the essence of their lived experiences with outdoor education. Participants were asked about their earliest memories of learning outdoors. The first conclusion is that the family played an important role in providing early learning experiences in the natural environment, which led to the identification of the themes "family experiences" and "free play."

The first finding was that participants indicated that the family played an important role in providing early learning experiences in the natural environment. Family was identified as a critical component of learning, whether the learning was in a traditional classroom, outdoors, experiential, or any other method. The data revealed themes about the importance of family and the importance of free play when students described the essence of their lived experiences with outdoor education.

Adam described the importance of his early experiences camping, fishing, and hunting with his family and how these experiences generated curiosity about the natural world. Adam described how members of his family served as role models that provided connections between his Native American culture and the environment through the use of generational stories and how his experiences with outdoor educational experiences helped built upon this cultural knowledge in order to expand his understanding of the environment and of himself. He attributed his successes to his strong family support. Harry, another Native American student described similar experiences.

The conceptual framework was based, in part, on the writings of Margolin (2005). Margolin identified experiential learning embedded in a culturally-relevant curriculum as critical to a successful pedagogy for Native American youth. In a conversation with one of the tribal elders at a reservation near the study site I was told that for learning to be lifelong and meaningful among Native American youth it must be learned by the heart, not by the head. The concept of learning as integral to being was inferred throughout the conversations with the two Native American participants who participated in this study. Both participants described the integral link their families and their culture had with the environment, both as a provider of resources such as deer for food and as a provider of spiritual connectedness. They both felt that, in part, a disengagement from the spiritual connectedness with nature was often seen in Native youth who were experiencing difficulties in finding success in school and in their community.

Betty described the freedom she had growing up on a family hobby farm. She was much younger than her siblings and grew up in a very solitary environment. She shared the importance of the animals on her farm fulfilling the role of friends and companions. During her childhood, she expressed sadness about her parents' remoteness as a result of alcohol addiction but described the power of nature in providing a healing milieu as she rebuilt a healthy relationship with her now sober parents. She described her relationship with her father:

I haven't known him any other way. When I was little, when you ask a kid what does the cow say and they say "Moo." What does a baby say, they say "Waa." Mom would say what does Daddy say and I would say "Mmm, whiskey." I didn't know, they laughed so I thought it was funny so I said it all the time. I didn't realize that it's not really a good thing. Now they're both 100% clean. My dad has found this new path. He's an amazing person, drinking or not. I love him to death. He's become very outdoorsy as well. He's been kayaking and canoeing more. He promises to take me along because I don't get very many opportunities to do that. To be able to do that, be able to get out there and kayak and canoe that would be awesome."

Betty was very proud of her new relationship with her father and talked about the times they sit on the porch, watching the animals in the yard. She talked extensively about the role that the outdoors played in building the bond with her father.

David reiterated the importance of the importance of the family and nature connection. His memories of early experiences are seasoned with references to outdoor activities like fishing and camping with his family, hunting with his grandfather, and logging with his grandfather and uncle. He stressed the peacefulness of spending time outdoor and how he uses those experiences to relieve the stress that is part of becoming an adult.

Carrie, Evan, and Fred had a different experience. While they also expressed some of the best outdoor times of their childhood were spent in free play, they had not been involved in the outdoor activities with family that the others had. They talked about how they spent much of their free time now with electronic media such as television, digital music, and their computers. Although Carrie and Evan were involved with school sports, they did not participate in voluntary, outside of school, experiences outdoors.

It would appear from the literature review that children spend a large percent of their day in artificial environments engaged in passive interactions with visual media such as television and the internet. This was a marked departure from previous generations in which it was common place for parents to command their children to go outside and play. This type of interaction with the natural environment was unstructured free play encouraging an independent sensory exploration of the child's world. As the literature review pointed out, most of the interactions adolescent children had with nature were highly-structured, adult-led activities.

Sternberg (1990) emphasized the role of culture in shaping the cultural values that formed a child's implicit knowledge. Based on Sternberg's theory, children without early outdoor experiences might not have the declarative and procedural knowledge necessary for academic success. A practical application of this finding could be found in school districts providing opportunities for family use of outdoor recreation facilities and the inclusion of family oriented activities in school planning.

Conclusion Two – Experiential Outdoor Learning is Beneficial to Learners

The second research question asked about students' recollections their outdoor educational experiences and the reasons why they recalled those experiences. The participants were asked to recall their recent experiences at the school forest. The second conclusion of this study was that the high quality, experiential, hands-on nature of the learning experience was the most beneficial characteristic of outdoor educational experiences which was indicated in the themes of personal growth and leadership identified from the findings.

The second finding was that participants indicated that the quality of the outdoor educational instruction was an important component in the positive perception of these experiences. The amount of time/depth of instruction was an important consideration to the quality of the learning. First experiences at the school forest can color all other experiences-- much like first impressions are so important. Participants did not see the school's interest in outdoor education being carried out in classroom instruction. The participants acknowledge great outdoor resources but don't see a lot of use of these resources. Students indicate that most school forest experiences are at the elementary level, few experiences are part of the high school curriculum and that this should be addressed.

The conceptual framework was based, in part, on the writings of Cobb (1977) and Gardner (2005). Cobb discussed the importance of a child's experience of nature in generating adult cognition and psychological well-being. The findings as detailed in section 4 support Cobb's contention. Adam, Betty, Carrie, David, Evan, and Harry discussed how the use of an outdoor educational experience provided an opportunity to explore concepts in depth, provided an opportunity to inquire and explore the observations they made during their experiences, and provided opportunities to connect family and cultural experiences with their educational experiences. These experiences are supported by the scholarly works of Gardner (2005) who promoted the idea of a naturalist intelligence, which he characterized as the ability to sense patterns and make connections in natural settings. The brain-based underpinnings of Gardner's naturalist intelligence are founded upon the natural affinity human beings have for their natural environment. This natural affinity was stronger in children than adults and involved sensory exploration along with creative expression. Responses that aligned with the feeling of well-being associated with a natural affinity for the natural environment were coded psychological well-being. The density of psychological well-being codes was one of the highest of all coded responses.

Adam described his first experience with outdoor education as being a field trip to the school forest. Although he does not remember much about the day, he remembers the fun of being outside, being able to run and being able to freely explore. Betty also remembered "the laid back part of it. It's not as strict. You can stand up, sit down whatever." Carrie had an uncomfortable experience with uncooperative weather. "It was raining out too. It was just really crappy weather. I don't know why we went out there. It was probably right after the snow all melted and it was rainy out so it was probably April, early April. It just sucked." Evan also reported negative experiences when they looked for water invertebrates and failed to find any. The early experiences of these participants were consistent with their description of their family experiences with nature. Participants that described extensive outdoor activities with their family tended to enjoy the messy part of outdoor education while the participants who had described few to no outdoor experiences with their family viewed the unpredictable nature of outdoor activities negatively.

The depth and quality of instruction associated with outdoor education was a concern of the participants, especially as they moved from elementary. "The time consuming part was all chop, chop we've got get there, do this. We didn't have much time to help them learn anything really" (Adam). Adam recalled that the most effective outdoor learning opportunities occurred when "you had the whole day to learn the one thing you were going to learn." He explained that "It was way easier to learn and concentrate on what we were going to do when we spent enough time on what we had to learn." When Betty was asked about the time she went to the school forest, she explained "We went out there a lot more when I was younger rather than now I wish we could get out there more. I haven't gone out in a few years." I asked her why she had not been involved in programs out at the school forest and she replied "I've had opportunities to go out there, but I don't like missing school to go out there because I'm not set to graduate and I'm having difficulties with math so I need to stay on that instead of going out. It would be more fun to go that route" (Betty). When asked to expound on her answer, she replied,

> It would be amazing if the teachers could get together. Or at least make it a little
>
> easier to miss school, make it an easier day, so you're not missing as much. If
>
> they could somehow get together. I guess that sounds cheesy, but to get them
>
> together so we can go out to the school forest. That'd be really nice. Even maybe
>
> just juniors and seniors because mainly that's who has classes together,
>
> senior/junior classes or something like that. It's a small school, we have 17 kids
>
> in our senior class, 20 kids, so it wouldn't be too difficult to have a couple classes
>
> out there with enough teachers supervising.

Greta reinforced the idea that even though the district provided outdoor educational experiences, the implementation was not there.

They spend all this money and they make it really great thing and they tell us about it, but then yet we only have a couple opportunities to actually use it. When we do ask or anything like that, it's 'No, no, no we have to do this'. Ok, great!

Carrie reiterated this idea when she talked about the value of outdoor educational experiences, "For students being able to learn outside, not just saying let's go outside and pick up rocks or something, but being able to go and be surrounded by a whole area that's specifically for the learning purpose is nice." Fred echoed the idea that outdoor educational experiences lacked depth of instruction and was used more as a stand-alone activity than as an integrated part of the curriculum. With an increased interest in environmental literacy (No Child Left Inside Coalition, 2009), a practical application of this finding could be found in school districts providing PK-12 professional development for educators in the field of outdoor education. Another application of this finding could be found in the encouragement of the formation of educational partnerships with recreational, governmental, and environmental agencies.

Conclusion Three –Freedom of Thought Encourages Creativity and Critical Thinking

The final research question asked about the ways in which students perceived outdoor educational experiences as being important to them in the future. Participants were asked for a description of the role the school forest played in their education and how their experiences would influence their future. The final conclusion of the study was that outdoor educational experiences provided a feeling of physical freedom and freedom of thought, which encouraged an increase in creativity and critical thinking skills which is reflected in the themes of cognitive freedoms and values.

The third finding was that participants indicated that outdoor educational instruction had a positive impact on the cognitive skills of the participants. Learning in the school forest improved cognition by creating a personal sense of freedom so thoughts were not confined to the walls of a classroom. Many students mentioned quiet as a reason for being outside. Sensory inputs in nature are less discordant with learning than the artificial sensory inputs in the classroom. "It's peaceful maybe. I don't know. It's isolated away from cell phones, computers, stuff like that. So we could think" (Fred). Several of the participants remarked on how the quiet found in nature helped them to focus on the noise of their environment. "When you actually spend just a few minutes being quiet, it's amazing how much more you can hear" (Harry). Adam brought the ability to quiet his mind back into the classroom. "You learn a lot when you sit and listen. It helps." Other participants also remarked on how sensory inputs helped them learn.

> Definitely you need to be quiet to observe everything around you in the wild. Just walking you see a lot, but sitting there listening, seeing, feeling the wind, you can definitely learn a lot more than just walking through the wild. There's so many more things to pick up on. Getting to hear the rustle of leaves way back then when you walk over there you can find what it is. It's different. (Carrie)

The natural environment seemed to provide a setting in which the participants were able to find the quiet necessary to receive the sensory inputs, which aided their cognitive processes.

The conceptual framework that structured this study was based, in part, on the writings of Carson (1965) and was supported by the findings discussed in section 4. Carson's (1965) work detailed the necessity of instilling what she referred to as a sense of wonder, which encouraged parents to provide opportunities for young children to experience the excitement of natural discoveries. A sense of wonder is an important part of building resilience against the "boredom and disenchantments of later years" (Carson, 1965, p. 54). Adam, Betty, Carrie, David, Evan, and Harry discussed the importance of leaving the four walls of the classroom in promoting their critical thinking ability. The freedom to explore their environment in order to analyze and synthesize the information learned inside the classroom was important to their ability to internalize a holistic concept relevant to their lives. One participant talked about the importance of the "laid back atmosphere where we can sit and get our butts dirty" (Betty).

In addition to the sensory benefits related to outdoor educational experiences, many of the participants discussed the value of the hands-on, experiential lessons in their cognitive processing. "I like hands-on. Getting out and doing what you learn about. Hands-on is my thing for everything" (Adam). All the other participants agreed on the value of experiential learning.

> It's definitely more open and people are different. Some people are more visual, some are more hands-on, some are more just listening and they got it. But, for people that are more hands-on and need to see what they're doing and be more interactive, like one-on-one or with the whole group, it's a good experience for people to go out there. (Betty)

Outdoor education is often synonymous with experiential education and encourages creativity, another frequently expressed cognitive benefit.

> We did a lot of arts and crafts out there, which I really enjoyed. We made baskets with bark and turkey feathers and stuff. I guess, just home life is, I know I keep

going back to that, but that's where it would affect me the most is what I would do in my free time. I love being out in the woods. I would probably have to thank being introduced to that at the school forest. (Betty)

When students are outdoors, they continually interact with nature and their inquisitive nature becomes inspired to explore their world. The fact that the learning is part of their world is part of the cognitive process.

Place-based education helps make learning relevant for students and was a continued theme throughout the participant responses. Participants found that taking skills they learned in their outdoor education programs into their community was powerful. "I'm cutting down old dead trees and just going and picking up recyclables and stuff like that for right now" (Adam). This participant talked about mentoring younger people to become more aware of the importance of recycling. Other participants have become more aware of how tourists treat the places that they have taken such pride in. "A lot of them who come up here just don't really care about it. They don't take care of anything, destroy it. Try to give them a better understanding to not destroy things, but just take care of it and it'll be around" (Evan). Many of the participants (Adam, Betty, Carrie, Evan, Greta) felt that the motivation to learn more about the natural environment increased their leadership skills so that they could make a difference in their community. These students were able to increase their cognitive skills to an evaluative level where they could develop opinion, judgments, and decisions. Evan summed up his knew understandings about the importance of community involvement with "You can't be a turtle all secluded" (Evan).

The importance of outdoor educational experiences in cognitive processes was summed up by one of the participants. "You learn a lot. You learn a lot out there. Every time you go out you learn something new" (David). Cognition, the process where we learn about our world, was a recurrent theme throughout the interview process.

> I learned a lot about trees. I didn't really know about trees. I figured a tree is a tree. I know we did a lot with studying trees - kinds of trees, how long it takes. An oak tree is only this big around, but it's almost 100 years old. I never really thought about it. (Fred)

Outdoor education emphasizes interpersonal and intrapersonal skills while enhancing independent, participatory learning (Hill, 2007; Priest & Gass, 1997; Zink & Burrows, 2006). Outdoor education emphasizes holistic learning and is focused on the physical, mental, social, emotional, spiritual, and environmental factors of a healthy self-esteem (Green & Kreuter, 2005; Sheinfeld-Gorin & Arnold, 2006). Outdoor educational experiences impact learning in positive ways. These experiences link important early learning experiences with family to quality educational experiences in formal education to increased cognitive skills in our recent high school graduates. A practical application of this finding is that school districts understand the importance of providing opportunities and outdoor classrooms for outdoor educational experiences.

Implication for Social Change

The implications for social change related to outdoor educational experiences were originally presented in section 1. Section 4 presented the participants' perceptions and stories related to the natural environment as an educational resource. The participants' stories help enrich the understanding of outdoor educational experiences.

The findings of this study are important to parents, classroom teachers, administrators, and students. This study contributes to social change in that it provides local and state educators with more information related to the investment in and importance of using outdoor classrooms and other natural settings.

Parents will find this study helpful as it clarifies the importance of providing opportunities for their children to participate in unstructured free play in outdoor settings. Young children spend little time outdoors and most of that time is spent in structured activities supervised by adults. The findings in section 4 demonstrate that what is important to young people is the free time they spend outside. Participants indicated that it was the time outdoors to hike, to bike, to play tag, to make up games, to explore, and to use their imaginations that made the longest-lasting impressions on them.

Teachers will find this study helpful as a catalyst to move beyond the four walls of their classroom. Students benefit when teachers utilize outdoor educational experiences as part of their instructional methodology. Participants in this study indicated that it was when teachers took them outside that they were freed from the constraints of learning the right answer and were able to physically and mentally explore alternative explanations for problems, whether those problems were posed by the teacher or posed by themselves. Participants in this study also indicated that they when their teachers took them outside, the learning became more effective because it was hands-on. In addition, the findings of this study may benefit teachers by providing evidence of the benefits of outdoor learning experiences so that this type of learning is supported by administration.

The phenomenological approach is also important to school district administrators as it clarifies the positive impact that investments in outdoor educational experiences have on students. This study provides a clear view of student perceptions of the value of outdoor educational experiences and the benefits of encouraging their teaching staff by supporting outdoor educational experiences and providing a location and facilities for outdoor educational experiences.

Finally, the findings of this study are important for students. The findings of this study contributed to the literature on the impact of outdoor experiences on student education. In this study, students identified their learning styles as grounded in experiential, hands-on opportunities that are culturally-relevant. The benefit of outdoor educational experiences manifests as a learning environment that includes place-based educational strategies, culturally-relevant, holistic educational strategies, and constructivist educational strategies reinforcing the naturalist intelligence as defined by Gardner (2005). As a result of this type of learning environment, the potential for academic success of students increases.

Recommendations for Action

Providing outdoor educational experiences for students is an interdisciplinary, experiential instructional approach. The stories of the participants illustrated the importance of outdoor educational experiences. Based on the findings of this study, the provision of outdoor classroom facilities and the provision of professional development opportunities to prepare teachers for the delivery of outdoor educational experiences are meaningful endeavors for school districts wanting to improve the rate of student success. Consequently, it is recommended that professional development be provided to help teachers feel comfortable and confidant in their ability to effectively use outdoor educational experiences as an educational strategy. Further, it is recommended that school districts explore opportunities to provide facilities for outdoor educational experiences.

Although providing outdoor educational experiences for students was externally supported by the study site's administration, this study found that it was not entrenched in the curricular structure of the district. This study indicated that participants found their secondary teachers to be unwilling to work together to enable students to take part in outdoor educational activities when those opportunities are offered. The participants felt they had to choose success in traditional secondary classrooms over participation in a learning opportunity at their school forest. The disconnect between these educational modalities guides my recommendation that school district administrators encourage secondary teachers to work collaboratively in interdisciplinary outdoor educational opportunities.

A few of the participants mentioned that they would have liked their outdoor educational experiences to explore content in more depth. They were concerned about the "chop, chop we've got get there, do this. We didn't have much time to learn anything really" (Adam). Therefore, another recommendation is that educators are offered professional development opportunities on how to incorporate outdoor educational experiences that provide in-depth experiences that encourage higher-level thinking skills.

A final recommendation is that school districts build opportunities for families to participate in school forest activities. Many of the participants recalled stories of participating in outdoor educational experiences with their families early in their early childhood and adolescence. The studies discussed in section 1 articulated a growing trend in indoor or structured outdoor activities such as soccer or baseball. Participants in this study expounded on the need for time to play outside during their youth. If school districts provided opportunities for parents to take their children outside for exploratory events sponsored by the school district, it may help provide the structured events parents prefer with the outdoor free play that the participants preferred. Dissemination of these recommendations resulted through the development of an executive summary provided to the superintendent of the study site and to the local site inspiring this study.

Recommendations for Further Study

This phenomenological study explored the essence of meaning in the lived experiences of high school seniors who had taken part in outdoor educational experiences. Due to the limited scope of this study, the results cannot be generalized to include the perceptions of all students in the school district or other districts across the state or other states in the country. For that reason, it is recommended that this study be replicated using a larger population of students who have participated in outdoor educational activities in other school districts. Another consideration would be to include students from rural and urban areas.

As discussed previously in the recommendations for action found in this section, teachers may lack knowledge and understanding of how to adequately infuse outdoor educational experiences into their curriculum. Following professional development, a subsequent study could be conducted to gather data for comparison about how students perceive school forest experiences conducted by adequately trained teachers.

An interesting area for further study might include looking at how student perceptions differ between outdoor educational experiences that involve longer periods of time including overnight stays at on-site lodges or tent camping and single day trips. This type of study could be helpful to school districts as they plan outdoor classroom infrastructure.

Reflections

Prior to conducting the interviews, I spent time in reflecting on my personal perceptions of outdoor educational experiences, both as a participant and as an instructor, in an effort to set aside my own opinions and bias. During the interviews, I refrained from commenting or sharing experiences with participants until they had answered the questions in the interview protocol. Having the interview protocol and the accompanying probes was very helpful in my efforts to stay neutral during the interview process. One revelation of the study was that students did not remember the intended learning outcomes of the outdoor experience, yet they did remember the sensory nature of the experience and the feeling of physical and mental freedom from the constraints of the classroom.

I found the involvement in this study to be personally challenging, yet exhilarating. The participants were willing and forthcoming about their experiences with outdoor education, both the positive and the negative, and how school districts could improve the experience for other students. As a result of this study, I have clarified my own views of outdoor educational experiences, in particular, as to how the experiences helped students gain higher-level thinking skills especially in the areas of creativity and leadership. The specific learning objectives were not as important as the overall results in which students felt free to explore alternative answers to questions that they themselves had generated.

Concluding Statement

The lack of empirical knowledge regarding students' lived experiences in outdoor educational activities along with the need of school districts to better understand the role of outdoor educational experiences served as problems for this study. As a result of the aforementioned problems, schools are investigating the use of outdoor classrooms as an educational resource for the improvement of education. In an effort to address this problem, I used the methodology of hermeneutic phenomenology in a search for a composite meaning of several individual's description of their lived experiences as interpreted by me. This study explored the essence of the lived experiences of eight students who had experienced outdoor education. Analyses revealed that students find value in their outdoor educational experiences.

Based on the analysis of the data, the value of outdoor educational experiences can be described in four statements. First, the participants in this study found that the success of outdoor educational experiences was rooted in their early experiences of outdoor free play. Second, the participants in this study felt that the sensory and experiential nature of outdoor educational experiences was an effective learning tool that helped them build leadership skills and find creative solutions to real-world problems. Third, the participants in this study felt that their outdoor educational experiences helped them make connections between what their culture and their formal education. Finally, participants in this study felt that the outdoor educational experiences would be helpful to them in the future because of the leadership skills and higher-level thinking skills that they had developed. The results of this study will help parents, teachers, and administrators understand the value of investing in outdoor educational experiences.

References

Adams, A., & Sveen, R. (2000). An holistic model of Bush Counseling: Cornerstones of practice. *Australian Journal of Outdoor Education, 5(*1). 28-39. Retrieved from http://www.galegroup.com

American Institute for Research. (2005). *Effects of outdoor education programs for children in California.* Retrieved from www.AIR.org

Anonymous. (2007). Students Explore Their Grande Passion. *Reclaiming Children and Youth, 16*(1), 7-8.

Annie E. Casey Foundation. (2009). *Kids count data book: Profiles of child well-being.* Retrieved from www.annieecaseyfoundation.org

Athman, J., & Monroe, M. C. (2004a). The effects of environment-based education on students' achievement motivation. *Journal of Interpretation Research 9(*1), 9 – 25. Retrieved from www.interpnet.com

Athman, J., & Monroe, M. C. (2004b). The effects of environment-based education on students' critical thinking skills and disposition toward critical thinking. *Environmental Education Research, 10(4),* 507 – 522. doi:10.1080/1350462042000291038

Muhr, T. (2004). *Atlas.ti 5.0 Users Manual.* Retrieved from www.atlas.ti.com

Barnett, M., Lord, C., Strauss, E., Rosca, C., Langford, H., Chavez, D., & Deni, L. (2006). Using the urban environment to engage youths in urban ecology field studies. *Journal of Environmental Education, 37*(2), 3-11. doi:10.3200/JOEE.37.2.3-11

Barnhardt, R. (2008). Creating a place for indigenous knowledge in education: The Alaska Native Knowledge Network. In D. A. Gruenewald & G. A. Smith (Eds.), *Place-based education in the global age* (pp. 5-27). New York: Lawrence Erlbaum Associates.

Barta, J., Abeyta, A., Gould, D., Galindo, E., Matt, G., Seaman, D., Voggesser, G. (2001). The mathematical ecology of the Shoshoni and implications for elementary mathematics education and the young learner. *Journal of American Indian Education, 40*(2), 1-27.

Bartosh, O., Ferguson, L., Tudor, M., & Taylor, C. (2009). Impact of environment-based teaching on student achievement: A study of Washington State Middle Schools. *Middle Grades Research Journal, 4*(4), 1-16.

Bartosh, O., Tudor, M., Taylor, C., & Ferguson, L. (2006). Improving WASL scores through environmental education: Is it possible? *Applied Environmental Education and Communication, 5(*3), 161 – 170.

Beard, C., & Wilson, J. P. (2006). *Experiential learning: A best practice handbook for educators and trainers.* Philadelphia, PA: Kogan Page, Limited.

Beaulieu, D. (2000). Comprehensive Reform and American Indian Education. *Journal of American Indian Education, 39*(2), 29-38.

Benard, B. (2004). *Resiliency: What we have learned.* San Francisco: WestEd.

Bialeschki, M. D. (2007). The three Rs for experiential education researchers. *Journal of Experiential Education, 29(*3), 366 - 368.

Black, K., & Lobo, M. (2008). A conceptual review of family resilience factors. *Journal of Family Nursing, 14*(33), 33-55. doi:10.1177/1074840707312237

Blair, D. (2009). The child in the garden: an evaluative review of the benefits of school
gardening. *The Journal of Environmental Education, 40(2)*, 15 – 38.
doi:10.3200/JOEE.40.2.15-38

Blumer, H. (1986). *Symbolic interactionism: Perspective and method.* Berkeley, CA:
University of California Press.

Bowman, N. (2003). Cultural differences of teaching and learning: A Native American
perspective participating in educational systems and organizations. *American
Indian Quarterly, 27*(1/2), 91-102. doi:10.1353/aiq.2004.0022

Broda, H. (2007). *Schoolyard enhanced learning: Using the outdoors as an instructional
tool, K-8.* Portland, ME: Stenhouse Publishers.

Bucknell, C., & Mannion, A. (Jan 2006). An outdoor education body of
knowledge. *Australian Journal of Outdoor Education*, 10, 1. p.39 (7). Retrieved
from http://find.galegroup.com

Burdette, H., & Whitaker, R. (2005). Resurrecting free play in young children: Looking
beyond fitness and fatness to attention, affiliation and affect. *Archives of
Pediatrics & Adolescent Medicine, 159*:46-50. Retrieved from
www.archpediatrics.com

Carson, R. (1956). *A sense of wonder.* New York: Harper and Row.

Cachelin, A., Paisley, K., & Blanchard, A. (2009). Using the significant life experience
framework to inform program evaluation: The Nature Conservancy's Wings &
Water Wetlands Education Program. *Journal of Environmental Education, 40*(2),
2-14. doi:10.3200/JOEE.40.2.2-14

Chawla, L. (2007, December). Childhood experiences associated with care for the natural world: A theoretical framework for empirical results. *Children, Youth & Environments, 17*(4), 144-170. Retrieved from www.colorado.edu/journals/cye

Chawla, L. (1999). Life paths into effective environmental action. *Journal of Environmental Education, 31*(1), 15. doi:10.1080/00958969909598628

Chen, G., & Weikart, L. (2008). Student background, school climate, school disorder, and student achievement: an empirical study of New York City's middle schools. *Journal of School Violence, 7*(4), 3-20. doi:10.1080/15388220801973813

Creswell, J. W. (2007). *Qualitative inquiry and research design: Choosing among five approaches* (2nd ed.). Thousand Oaks, CA: Sage Publications.

Creswell, J. W. (2003). *Research design: Qualitative, quantitative, and mixed methods approaches* (2nd ed.). Thousand Oaks, CA: Sage Publications.

Cobb, E. (1977). *The Ecology of Imagination in Childhood.* Putnam, CT: Spring Publications.

Cole, A. (2007, Winter). Expanding the field: Revisiting environmental education principles through multidisciplinary frameworks. *The Journal of Environmental Education*, 38(2), 35-44. doi:10.3200/JOEE.38.1.35-46

College Board, N. (1999, January 1). Reaching the top: A report of the National Task Force on Minority High Achievement. (ERIC Document Reproduction Service No. ED435765)

Connecticut Department of Environmental Protection. (2009). No Child Left Inside. Retrieved from http://www.nochildleftinside.org/learn/

Connell-Szasz, M. (1999). *Education and the American Indian* (3rd ed.). University of New Mexico Press. (Original work published 1974)

Davis, B., Rea, T., & Waite, S. (July 2006). The special nature of the outdoors: its contribution to the education of children aged 3-11. *Australian Journal of Outdoor Education*, 10, 2. p.3(10). Retrieved from http://find.galegroup.com

Davis, B., & Waite, S. (2005). Forest Schools: An evaluation of the opportunities and challenges in early years final report. Retrieved from http://www.edu.plymouth.ac.uk

Dewey, J. (1916). *Democracy and education: An introduction to the philosophy of education*. New York, NY: Cosimo, Inc.

Dewey, J. (1938). *Experience & education.* New York, NY: Touchstone by Simon and Schuster.

Dilthey, W. (1985). *Poetry and Experience.* Princeton, NJ: Princeton University Press.

Deloria, V., & Wildcat, D. (2001). *Power and Place: Indian Education in American.* Golden, CO: Fulcrum Resources.

Demmert Jr., W. (2005, February). The influences of culture on learning and assessment among Native American students. *Learning Disabilities Research & Practice (Blackwell Publishing Limited)*, 20(1), 16-23. doi: 10.1111/j.1540-5826.2005.00116.x

Doolittle, P. (1995, January 1). *Understanding cooperative learning through Vygotsky's Zone of Proximal Development.* (ERIC Document Reproduction Service No. ED384575).

Dyment, J. (2005). Gaining ground: The power and potential of school ground greening in the Toronto District School Board: Evergreen. Retrieved December 20, 2008 from http:www.evergreen.ca/en/lg/gaining_ground.pdf

Ebersole, M., & Worster, A. (2007, Winter). Sense of place in teacher preparation courses: place-based and standards-based education. *Delta Kappa Gamma Bulletin, 73*(2), 19-24. Retrieved from www.deltakappagamma.net

Education, S. (2004, April 2). Our voice, your voice, one voice: Nurturing American Indian families for school success. *North Carolina Department of Public Instruction*, (ERIC Document Reproduction Service No. ED484679)

Ernst, J., & Monroe, M. (2006, July). The effects of environment-based education on students' critical thinking skills and disposition toward critical thinking. *Environmental Education Research, 12*(3/4), 429-443. doi:10.1080/13504620600942998

Faber Taylor, A., & Kuo, F. (2008). Children with attention deficits concentrate better after a walk in the park. *Journal of Attention Disorders Online First.* doi:10.1177/1087054708323000

Faber Taylor, A., Kuo, F., & Sullivan, W. (2002). Views of nature and self-discipline: Evidence from inner city children. *Journal of Environmental Psychology*, 22, 49-63.

Farmer, J., Knapp, D., & Benton, G. (2007). An elementary environmental education field trip: Long term effects on ecological/environmental knowledge and attitude development. *Journal of Environmental Education* 38(3), 33-42. doi:10.3200/JOEE.38.3.33-42

Fixico, D. (2003). *The American Indian Mind in a Linear World*. New York: Routledge.

Foley, D. (2005). Elusive prey: John Ogbu and the search for a grand theory of academic disengagement. *International Journal of Qualitative Studies in Education, 18(*5), 643-657. doi: 10.1080/09518390500224986

Foran, A. (2005, September). The experience of pedagogic intensity in outdoor education. *Journal of Experiential Education*, *28*(2), 147-163.

Fram, M., Miller-Cribbs, J., & Van Horn, L. (2007). Poverty, race, and the contexts of achievement: Examining educational experiences of children in the U.S. south. *Social Work, 52(*4), 309-319.

Freire, P. (2008). *Pedagogy of the Oppressed.* (30th ed.). New York: Continuum.

Gadamer, H.-G. (1998). *Truth and method* (2nd ed.). New York: Continuum. (Original work published 1960.)

Gardner, H. (2005). *Multiple lenses on the mind.* Paper presented at ExpoGestion Conference. http://www.howardgardner.com

Garmezy, N. (1991). Resiliency and vulnerability to adverse developmental outcomes associated with poverty. *The American Behavioral Scientist. 34*(4), 416-430. doi:10.1177/0002764291034004003

Gibson, M. (2005). Promoting academic engagement among minority youth: implications from John Ogbu's Shaker Heights ethnography. *International Journal of Qualitative Studies in Education, 18(*5), 581-603. doi: 10.10800/09518390500224853

Gillham, B. (2005). *Interviewing the range of techniques.* New York: Open University Press.

Giorgi, A. (2006). Concerning Variations in the Application of the Phenomenological Method. *Humanistic Psychologist, 34*(4), 305-319. doi:10.1207/s15473333thCarrie404_2

Goldsmith, P. A. (2004). Schools' racial mix, students' optimism, and the black-white and Latino-white achievement gaps. *Sociology of Education, 77(*2):121-147. doi:10.1177/003804070407700202

Gordon, K. (1995). Self-concept and motivational patterns of resilient African American high school students. *Journal of Black Psychology, 21*, 239-255. Retrieved January 23, 2009, doi:10.1177/0095784950213003

Green, L., & Kreuter, M. (2005). *Health program planning: An educational and ecological approach.* New York: McGraw-Hill

Gruenewald, D. (2005, October). Accountability and collaboration: Institutional barriers and strategic pathways for place-based education. *Ethics, Place and Environment*, 8(3), 261-283. doi: 10.1080/13668790500348208

Gulpinar, M. (2005, November). The principles of brain-based learning and constructivist Models in education. *Educational Sciences: Theory & Practice*, 5(2), 299-306. Retrieved from www.edam.com

Haas, T., & Nachtigal, P. (1998). *Place value: An educator's guide to good literature on rural lifeways, environments, and purposes of education.* Charleston, WV: ERIC Clearinghouse on Rural Education and Small Schools.

Hall, M. (2007). Mentoring the natural way: Native American approaches to education. *Reclaiming Children & Youth, 16*(1), 14-16.

Hankes, J. (1996, April 1). *Investigating the Correspondence between Native American Pedagogy and Constructivist Based Instruction*. (ERIC Document Reproduction Service No. ED401-86).

Hatch, J. A. (2002). *Doing Qualitative Research in Education Settings*. Albany, NY: State University of New York Press.

Henwood, K., & Pidgeon, N. (1994). Beyond the qualitative paradigm: A framework for introducing diversity within qualitative psychology. *Journal of Community & Applied Social Psychology, 4*, 225-238. doi:10.1002/casp.2450040403

Hermes, M. (2000). The scientific method, Nintendo, and Eagle feathers: rethinking the meaning of `culture-based' curriculum at an Ojibwe tribal school. *International Journal of Qualitative Studies in Education (QSE)*, *13*(4), 387. doi:10.1080/095183900413340

Hill, N. (2007). Wilderness therapy as a treatment modality for at-risk youth: A primer for mental health counselors. *Journal of Mental Health Counseling, 29*(4), 338-349.

Hofferth, S., & Sandberg, J. (2001). Changes in American children's time, 1981-1997. In S.L. Hofferth & T.J. Owens (Eds.), *Children at the Millennium: Where Have We Come From, Where Are We Going?* New York: JAI.

Holt, M. (2005). The slow school: An idea whose time has come? In M. K. Stone & Z. Barlow (Eds.), *Ecological Literacy: Educating Our Children for a Sustainable World*. San Francisco: Cassirer Club Books.

Hubball, H., & West, D. (2009). Learning-centered planning strategies in outdoor

    education programs: Enhancing participation and self-directed learning. *Strategies*

    (08924562), *23*(1), 25-27.

Husserl, E. (1970). *The crisis of the European sciences and transcendental*

    phenomenology. (D. Carr, trans.). Evanston, IL: Northwestern University Press.

Hyun, E. (2000, April). *Ecological human brain and young children's naturalist*

    intelligence from the perspective of developmentally and culturally appropriate

    practice. (ERIC Document Reproduction Service No. ED440749)

Kellert, S. (2002). Experiencing nature: Affective, cognitive, and evaluative development

    in children. In P. Kahn, Jr. & S. Kellert (Eds.), *Children and nature:*

    Psychological, sociocultural, and evolutionary investigations (pp. 117-151),

    Cambridge, MS: The MIT Press.

Kellert, S. (2005). *Building for life: Designing and understanding the human-nature*

    connection. Washington DC: Island Press.

Klug, B. J., & Whitfield, P. T. (2003). *Widening the circle: Culturally relevant pedagogy*

    for American Indian children. New York, NY: RoutledgeFalmer.

Knapp, C. E. (2008). Place-based curricular and pedagogical models: My adventures in

    teaching through community contexts. In D. A. Gruenewald & G. A. Smith

    (Eds.), *Place-based education in the global age* (pp. 5-27). New York, NY:

    Lawrence Erlbaum Associates.

Knapp, C., & ERIC Clearinghouse on Rural Education and Small Schools, C. (1996).

    Just beyond the Classroom: Community Adventures for Interdisciplinary

    Learning. Retrieved from ERIC database.

Laverty, S. M. (2003). Hermeneutic phenomenology and phenomenology: A comparison of historical and methodological considerations. *International Journal of Qualitative Methods, 2*(3). Article 3. Retrieved from http://www.ualberta.ca/~iiqm/backissues/2_3final/html/laverty.html

Lester, S., & Maudsley, M. (2006). Play, naturally: A review of children's natural play. *Children's Play Council*. Retrieved December 29, 2008 from http://www.playday.org.uk

Leveque, D. (1994). Cultural and parental influences on achievement among Native American students in Barstow Unified School District. Retrieved from ERIC database.

Lew, J. (2006). Burden of acting neither white nor black: Asian American identities and achievement in urban schools. *The Urban Review 38(*5), pp. 335 – 352. doi:10.1007/s11256-006-0040-8

Lincoln, Y. S., & Guba, E. G. (1985). *Naturalistic Inquiry*. Newbury Park, CA: Sage Publications.

Louv, R. (2008). *Last child in the woods: Saving our children from nature-deficit disorder.* Chapel Hills, NC: Algonquin Books.

Margolin, (2005). Indian pedagogy: A look at traditional California Indian teaching techniques. In Orr, D. W. & Stone, M. K. (eds.), *Ecological literacy: Education our children for a sustainable world. (pp. 67 – 79).* San Francisco, CA: Sierra Club Books.

Marks, A., & Coll, C. (2007, May). Psychological and demographic correlates of early academic skill development among American Indian and Alaska Native youth: A growth modeling study. *Developmental Psychology, 43*(3), 663-674. doi:10.1037/0012-1649.43.3.663

Matsuoka, R. H. (2008). High school landscapes and student performance. (doctoral dissertation, University of Michigan, 2008). Available from ProQuest Dissertations and Thesis database. (Publication No. AAT 1563343).

McCombs, B. L. (2000). Reducing the achievement gap. *Society, 37(*5), 29. doi:10.1007/s12115-000-1034-x

McGee, G. W. (2004). Closing the achievement gap: Lessons from Illinois's Golden Spike high-poverty high performing schools. *Journal of Education for Students Placed At Risk, 9(*2), 97-125. Retrieved from www.csos.jhu.edu

McInerney, D., & McInerney, V. (2000, April 1). A longitudinal qualitative study of school motivation and achievement. (ERIC Document Reproduction Service No. ED441815)

Merriam, S. B., & Associates. (2002). *Qualitative research in practice.* San Francisco, CA: Jossey-Bass.

Messick, S. (1992). Multiple intelligences or multilevel intelligence? Selective emphasis on distinctive properties of hierarchy: On Gardner's Frames of Mind and Steinberg's Beyond IQ in the context of theory and research on the structure of human abilities. *Psychological Inquiry, 3*(4), 365. doi:10.1207/s15327965pli0304_20

Monroe, M. C., Randall, J., & Crisp, V. (2001). Improving student achievement with environmental education. Retrieved December 28, 2009 from http://edis.ifas.ufl.edu/fr114.

Morales, E. (2008a). Academic resilience in retrospect: Following up a decade later. *Journal of Hispanic Higher Education.* 7(3), 228-248. doi:10.1177/153819270831719

Morales, E. (2008b). A focus on hope: Toward a more comprehensive theory of academic resiliency among at-risk minority students. *The Journal of At-risk Issues, 14*(1), 23-32. Retrieved from www.dropoutprevention.org

Moran, S., Kornhaber, K., & Gardner, H. (2006). Orchestrating multiple intelligences. *Educational Leadership, 64*(1), 22-27. Retrieved from www.ascd.org

Moustakas, C. (1994). *Phenomenological Research Methods.* Thousand Oaks, CA: Sage.

National Research Council (2003). *Engaging schools: Fostering high school students' motivation to learn.* Washington, DC: National Academies of Science Press.

Nelson, K., Simons, L., Swanson, E., & Ohio Univ., A. (2003, January 1). *Research Issues for Mathematics Education in Rural Communities: Focus on Native Americans. Working Paper.* . (ERIC Document Reproduction Service No. ED478056)

Nelson-Barber, S., & Estrin, E. (1995, January 1). Bringing Native American perspectives to mathematics and science teaching. *Theory into Practice*, 34(3), 174-185. doi:10.1080/00405849509543677

No Child Left Inside Coalition. (2009). Retrieved from http://www.cbf.org

Norman, N., Jennings, A., Wahl, L. (2006). *The impact of environmentally-related education on academic achievement: A literature survey.* Berkley, CA: Community Resources for Science.

Ogbu, J. (2004). Collective identity and the burden of "acting white" in black history, community and education. *The Urban Review, 36(*1), 1-35. doi:10.1023/B:URRE.0000042734.83194.f6

Patton, M. (2002). *Qualitative evaluation and research methods* (3rd ed.). Thousand Oaks, CA: Sage.

Payne, R. (1996). *A framework for understanding poverty*. Highlands, TX: aha! Process, Inc.

Pewewardy, C. (2002). Learning styles of American Indian/Alaska Native student: A review of the literature and implications for practice. *Journal of American Indian Education*, 41(3), 22-56. Retrieved from www.jaie.asu.edu

Priest, S. (1986). Redefining outdoor education: A matter of many relationships. *Journal of Environmental Education, 7(*3), 13-15.

Priest, S., & Gass, M. (1997). *Effective leadership in adventure programming*. Retrieved from ERIC database.

Prince, D., Pepper, K., & Brocato, K. (2006, August). The importance of making the well-being of children in poverty a priority. *Early Childhood Education Journal, 34*(1), 21-28. doi:10.1007/s10643-006-0118-7

Public Policy Institute of California. (2007, September). *Just the facts: California's youth and outdoor activities*. Retrieved December 8, 2008 from http://www.ppic.org

Reyhner, J., & Eder, J. (2004). *American Indian Education: A History*. Norman, OK: University of Oklahoma Press.

Rural School and Community Trust. (2003, June 1). *Engaged Institutions: Impacting the Lives of Vulnerable Youth through Place-Based Learning.* (ERIC Document Reproduction Service No. ED481278)

Schein, E. H. (2003). On dialogue, culture, and organizational learning. *Reflections, 4(*4), 27-38. doi:10.1162/152417303322004184

Sheinfeld-Gorin, S., & Arnold, J. (2006). *Health Promotion in Practice.* San Francisco, CA: Jossey –Bass.

Smith, E. (2006). The strength-based counseling model. *The Counseling Psychologist 34*(1), 13-79. doi:10.1177/0011000005277018

Sobel, D. (2005). *Place-based Education.* Great Barrington, MA: The Orion Society.

Solin, J. (2007). Doing what works, teaching what matters: Utilizing school forests. *Association of Wisconsin School Administrators E-Update, 30(*1), 14-17. Retrieved from www.awsa.org

Sparks, S. (2000). Classroom and curriculum accommodations for Native American students. *Intervention in School and Clinic*, 35(5), 259-263. doi:10.1177/105345120003500501

Starnes, B. (2006). What we don't know "can" hurt them: White teachers, Indian children. *Phi Delta Kappan, 87*(5), 384-392.

Sternberg, R., Okagaki, L., & Jackson, A. (1990, September). Practical intelligence for success in school. *Educational Leadership, 48*(1), 35-39. Retrieved from www.ascd.org

Stevenson, R. L., & Kincade, T. (1999). *A child's garden of verses a collection of scriptures, prayers & poems.* Nashville, TN: Tommy Nelson Inc.

Swarbrick, N., Eastwood, G., & Tutton, K. (2004). Self-esteem and successful interaction as part of the forest school project. *Support for Learning, 19*(3), 142-146. doi:10.1111/j.0268-2141.2004.00337.x.

Taylor, A., Kuo, F., & Sullivan, W. (2001). Coping with ADD: The surprising connection to green play settings. *Environment and Behavior, 33*(1), 54-77. doi:10.1177/00139160121972864.

Tesch, R. (1990). *Qualitative research: Analysis types and software tools.* London: Falmer.

Tyson, K. (2002). Weighing in: Elementary-age students and the debate on attitudes toward school among black students. *Social Forces, 80(*4), 1157-1189. doi:10.1353/sof.2002.0035

Uhlik, K. S. (2009). A conceptual inquiry into the integration of sacred nature, society, and leadership in outdoor recreation and experiential education programs. *Journal of Experiential Education, 32(*2), 103- 120.

United States Environmental Protection Agency. (2009). *Environmental education.* Retrieved from http://www.epa.gov/education

Van Manen, M. (1990). *Researching Lived Experience.* Albany, NY: State University of New York Press.

Vandewater, E., Rideout, V., Wartella, E., Huang, X., Lee, J., & Shim, M. (2007). Digital childhood: Electronic media and technology use among infants, toddlers, and preschoolers. *Pediatrics, 119*(5), e1006-e1015, doi:10.1542/peds.2006-1804

Vygotsky, L. (1986). *Thought and Language.* Cambridge, MA: The MIT Press.

Walden University. (2009). *Human research protection training course requirements.* Retrieved from http://sylvan.live.ecollege.com/

Wanat, C. (2006). Qualitative Research, History, Theories, Issues. *Encyclopedia of Educational Leadership and Administration.* SAGE Publications. Retrieved from http://sage-ereference.com

Wells, N., & Lekies, K. (2006). Nature and the life course: pathways from childhood nature experiences to adult environmentalism. *Children, Youth, and Environments, 16*(1), 1-24. Retrieved from www.colorado.edu/journals/cye

Wells, N., & Evans, G. (2003). Nearby nature: A buffer of life stress among rural children. *Environment and Behavior, 35*(3), 311-330. doi:10.1177/0013916503035003001

Werner, E., & Smith, R. (1992). *Overcoming the odds: High risk children from birth to adulthood.* New York: Cornell University Press.

Wilson, E. O. (1984). *Biophilia.* Cambridge, MA: Harvard University Press.

Wilson, E. O. (1998). *Consilience: The Unity of Knowledge.* New York: Vintage Books.

WINSS Successful School Guide. (n. d.). Retrieved December 28, 2008, from Wisconsin Department of Public Instruction Web site: www.dpi.state.wi.us

Zink, R., & Burrows, L. (2006). Foucault on Camp: What Does His Work Offer Outdoor Education? *Journal of Adventure Education & Outdoor Learning, 6*(1), 39-50. doi:10.1080/14729670685200731

Appendix A: Interview Protocol

Interview Protocol

Purpose: To put the experience in context

1. What is your earliest memory of learning something outdoors?

2. What do you recall about your first experience at the school forest?

Purpose: To gather details of the school forest experience

3. What do you recall about your most recent experience at the school forest?

4. Can you think of any times when you have applied something you learned at the school forest to your school work?

Purpose: To reflect on the school forest experience

5. How would you describe the role of the school forest in your education?

6. How do you see yourself using experiences at the school forest in your future?

Probes to use with each question (as needed)

To get more details . . .

- When did that happen?

- Who else was involved?

- Where were you during that time?

- What was your involvement in that situation?

- How did that come about?

- Where did it happen?

- How did you feel about that?

To elaborate . . .

- Would you elaborate on that?

- Could you say some more about that?

- That's helpful. I'd appreciate if you could give me more detail.

- I'm beginning to get the picture: but some more examples might help.

To clarify . . .

- You said X. What do you mean by X?

- What you're saying now is very important, and I want to make sure that I get it down exactly the way you mean it: please explain some more

Appendix B: Consent Forms

Student Assent Form

You are invited to take part in a research study of your perceptions of your outdoor educational experiences at the school forest. You were chosen for the study because you are a recent high school graduate and you participated in the outdoor experiences provided by the school.

This study is being conducted by Cynthia Edlund, who is a doctoral student at Walden University.

Background Information:
The purpose of this study is to understand what you think about your outdoor educational experiences at the school forest.

Procedures:
If you agree to be in this study, you will be asked to:
- Participate in an initial interview that will last approximately one hour.
- Interviews will be audio recorded.
- Participate in follow-up interviews, as needed.

Voluntary Nature of the Study:
Your participation in this study is voluntary. This means that everyone will respect your decision of whether or not you want to be in the study. No one at XXX will treat you differently if you decide not to be in the study. If you decide to join the study now, you can still change your mind during the study. If you feel stressed during the study you may stop at any time. You may skip any questions that you feel are too personal. There is no penalty for discontinuing your participation in the study.

Risks and Benefits of Being in the Study:
The risks to you are minimal and would be limited to not feeling comfortable answering certain questions. If you do not want to answer a question during the interview, you don't have to. The benefits include better understanding your goals and what is important to you. Benefits for schools are that you may help educators understand the role of outdoor educational experiences on student achievement.

Compensation:
There is no compensation for participants in this study.

Confidentiality:
Any information you provide was kept confidential. The researcher will not use your information for any purposes outside of this research project. Also, the researcher will not include your name or anything else that could identify you in any reports of the study.

Contacts and Questions:
You may ask any questions you have now. Or if you have questions later, you may contact the researcher via phone at 715-362-1847 or email at cynthia.edlund@waldenu.edu. If you want to talk privately about your rights as a participant, you can call Dr. Leilani Endicott. She is the Walden University representative who can discuss this with you. Her phone number is 1-800-925-3368, extension 1210. Walden University's approval number for this study is **07-09-10-0355340** and it expires on **July 8, 2011.**

The researcher will give you a copy of this form to keep.

Statement of Consent:

I have read the above information and I feel I understand the study well enough to make a decision about my involvement. By signing below, I am agreeing to the terms described above.

Printed Name of Participant

Date of consent

Participant's Written Signature

Researcher's Written Signature

Parental Consent Form

Your child is invited to take part in a research study of their perceptions of their outdoor educational experiences at the school forest. Your child was chosen for the study because your child is a recent high school graduate.

This study is being conducted by Cynthia Edlund, who is a doctoral student at Walden University.

Background Information:
The purpose of this study is to understand what your child thinks about the outdoor educational experiences at the school forest.

.

Procedures:
If you agree to let your child be in this study, your child will be asked to:
- Participate in an initial interview that will last approximately one hour.
- Interviews will be audio recorded.
- Participate in follow-up interviews, as needed.

Voluntary Nature of the Study:
Your child's participation in this study is voluntary. This means that everyone will respect your decision of whether or not you want your child to be in the study. No one at XXX will treat you or your child differently if you decide not to be in the study. If you decide to consent to the study now, you or your child can still change your minds during the study. Any child who feels stressed during the study may stop at any time. Children may also skip any questions that they feel are too personal. There is no penalty for discontinuing participation in the study.

Risks and Benefits of Being in the Study:
The risks to your child are minimal and would be limited to not feeling comfortable answering certain questions. If your child does not want to answer a question during the interview, they don't have to.

Benefits for schools are that you may help educators understand the role of outdoor educational experiences on student achievement.

Compensation:
There is no compensation for participants in this study.

Confidentiality:
Any information your child provides was kept confidential. The researcher will not use your child's information for any purposes outside of this research project. Also, the researcher will not include your child's name or anything else that could identify your child in any reports of the study.

Contacts and Questions:
You may ask any questions you have now. Or if you have questions later, you may contact the researcher via phone at 715-362-1847 or email at Cynthia.edlund@waldenu.edu. If you want to talk privately about your rights as a participant, you can call Dr. Leilani Endicott. She is the Walden University representative who can discuss this with you. Her phone number is 1-800-925-3368, extension 1210. Walden University's approval number for this study is **07-09-10-0355340** and it expires on **July 8, 2011.**

The researcher will give you a copy of this form to keep.

Statement of Consent:

I have read the above information and I feel I understand the study well enough to make a decision about my involvement. By signing below, I am agreeing to the terms described above.

Printed Name of Participant   _____

Printed Name of Parent   _____

Date of consent

Parent's Written Signature   _____

Researcher's Written Signature   _____

                                          _____

Student Consent Form

You are invited to take part in a research study of your perceptions of your outdoor educational experiences at the school forest. You were chosen for the study because you are a recent high school graduate and you participated in the outdoor experiences provided by the school.

This study is being conducted by Cynthia Edlund, who is a doctoral student at Walden University.

Background Information:
The purpose of this study is to understand what you think about your outdoor educational experiences at the school forest.
.
Procedures:
If you agree to be in this study, you will be asked to:
- Participate in an initial interview that will last approximately one hour.
- Interviews will be audio recorded.
- Participate in follow-up interviews, as needed.

Voluntary Nature of the Study:
Your participation in this study is voluntary. This means that everyone will respect your decision of whether or not you want to be in the study. No one at XXX will treat you differently if you decide not to be in the study. If you decide to join the study now, you can still change your mind during the study. If you feel stressed during the study you may stop at any time. You may skip any questions that you feel are too personal. There is no penalty for discontinuing your participation in this study.

Risks and Benefits of Being in the Study:
The risks to you are minimal and would be limited to not feeling comfortable answering certain questions. If you do not want to answer a question during the interview, you don't have to. The benefits include better understanding your goals and what is important to you. Benefits for schools are that you may help educators understand the role of outdoor educational experiences on student achievement.

Compensation:
There is no compensation for participants in this study.

Confidentiality:
Any information you provide was kept confidential. The researcher will not use your information for any purposes outside of this research project. Also, the researcher will not include your name or anything else that could identify you in any reports of the study.

Contacts and Questions:
You may ask any questions you have now. Or if you have questions later, you may contact the researcher via phone at 715-362-1847 or email at cynthia.edlund@waldenu.edu. If you want to talk privately about your rights as a participant, you can call Dr. Leilani Endicott. She is the Walden University representative who can discuss this with you. Her phone number is 1-800-925-3368, extension 1210. Walden University's approval number for this study is **07-09-10-0355340** and it expires on **July 8, 2011.**

The researcher will give you a copy of this form to keep.

Statement of Consent:

I have read the above information and I feel I understand the study well enough to make a decision about my involvement. By signing below, I am agreeing to the terms described above.

Printed Name of Participant
Date of consent   _____

Participant's Written Signature   _____

Researcher's Written Signature   _____

Site Permission

Elcho School District
N11268 Antigo Street
Elcho, WI 54428

March 8, 2010

Dear Mrs. Edlund,

Based on my review of your research proposal, I give permission for you to conduct the study entitled Student Perceptions of Outdoor Educational Experiences with in Elcho High School. As part of this study, I authorize you to interview high school seniors for the purposes of data collection. Individuals' participation will be voluntary and at their own discretion. We reserve the right to withdraw from the study at any time if our circumstances change.

I confirm that I am authorized to approve research in this setting.

I understand that the data collected will remain entirely confidential and may not be provided to anyone outside of the research team without permission from the Walden University IRB.

Sincerely,

Mr. Bill Fisher
District Superintendent

Transcriptionist Confidentiality Agreement

Name of Signer:

During the course of my activity in transcribing data for this research: "Student Perceptions of Outdoor Educational Experiences"

I will have access to information, which is confidential and should not be disclosed. I acknowledge that the information must remain confidential, and that improper disclosure of confidential information can be damaging to the participant.

By signing this Confidentiality Agreement I acknowledge and agree that:

1. I will not disclose or discuss any confidential information with others, including friends or family.
2. I will not in any way divulge, copy, release, sell, loan, alter or destroy any confidential information except as properly authorized.
3. I will not discuss confidential information where others can overhear the conversation. I understand that it is not acceptable to discuss confidential information even if the participant's name is not used.
4. I will not make any unauthorized transmissions, inquiries, modification or purging of confidential information.
5. I agree that my obligations under this agreement will continue after termination of the job that I will perform.
6. I understand that violation of this agreement will have legal implications.
7. I will only access or use systems or devices I'm officially authorized to access and I will not demonstrate the operation or function of systems or devices to unauthorized individuals.

Signing this document, I acknowledge that I have read the agreement and I agree to comply with all the terms and conditions stated above.

Signature: Date:

Peer Reviewer Confidentiality Agreement

Name of Signer:

During the course of my activity as a peer reviewer for the research: "Student Perceptions of Outdoor Educational Experiences"

I will have access to information, which is confidential and should not be disclosed. I acknowledge that the information must remain confidential, and that improper disclosure of confidential information can be damaging to the participant.

By signing this Confidentiality Agreement I acknowledge and agree that:

1. I will not disclose or discuss any confidential information with others, including friends or family.
2. I will not in any way divulge, copy, release, sell, loan, alter or destroy any confidential information except as properly authorized.
3. I will not discuss confidential information where others can overhear the conversation. I understand that it is not acceptable to discuss confidential information even if the participant's name is not used.
4. I will not make any unauthorized transmissions, inquiries, modification or purging of confidential information.
5. I agree that my obligations under this agreement will continue after termination of the job that I will perform.
6. I understand that violation of this agreement will have legal implications.
7. I will only access or use systems or devices I'm officially authorized to access and I will not demonstrate the operation or function of systems or devices to unauthorized individuals.

Signing this document, I acknowledge that I have read the agreement and I agree to comply with all the terms and conditions stated above.

Signature: **Date:**

Appendix C: Codes

Code	Meaning
EMEM	Earliest memory
FEXP	First experience at school forest
REXP	Most recent experience at school forest
APPL	Application of lessons
ROLE	Role of school forest in education
USE	Use of experiences in the future
HOL	Holistic - Interdisciplinary
EXPLEARN	Experiential Learning
NA	Native American Learning
COG	Cognition
CRIT	Critical Thinking
PSYCH	Psychological well-being
CREAT	Creative Expression
PLACEB	Place-based
LEAD	Building Leadership Skills
PGROWTH	Personal Growth
SENSORY	Sensory
SFREE	Sense of Freedom

Curriculum Vitae

Cynthia Edlund

Education
Walden University, Minneapolis, MN   2010
Doctorate of Education in Teacher as Leader
- Doctoral Study: Student Perceptions of Outdoor Educational Experiences

University of Wisconsin – Stevens Point, Stevens Point, WI   2002
Master of Science in Natural Resources; Environmental Education Emphasis

Colorado State University, Pueblo, CO   1989
Bachelor of Science, with Distinction

Professional Certification
Wisconsin Department of Public Instruction
License: 6 – 12 Science, Endorsements: Chemistry, Broadfield, and Biology/Life Science
Professional Development Plan Team Member Certification   2005

Professional Affiliations
- National Education Association
- Wisconsin Society of Science Teachers
- National Science Teachers Association
- Alpha Epsilon Xi Chapter of Kappa Delta Pi International Honor Society in Education

Professional Experience
Crandon High School, Crandon, WI   1996 – Present
Educator – Biology, Environmental Science, and Physical Science

Project WET, Leopold Education Project, Project Learning Tree,
Project Wild   2006 – Present
Facilitator

University of Wisconsin – Stevens Point
Adjunct Faculty – Wisconsin K-12 Energy Education Program   2008 – Present

Las Animas High School, Las Animas, CO
Educator –Biology, Physical Science, and Chemistry   1989 – 1996

Additional Experience
Hovind Family School Forest, Crandon, WI
School Forest Coordinator   2005 – Present

State School Forest / LEAF Advisory Committee   2007 – Present

Wisconsin Society of Science Teachers
Conference Committee Co-Chair, Program Chair   2009
Professional Development Committee Chair   2002 – 2006
Professional Development Committee   1997 – 2006
Secretary   2003 – 2005

School District of Crandon, Crandon, WI
Program Coordinator – New Teacher Mentor Program   2003 – 2006

CPSIA information can be obtained
at www.ICGtesting.com
Printed in the USA
LVIW021517211012

303796LV00010B